D0944256

THE MAN GOD USES

THE MAN GOD USES

BY

OSWALD J. SMITH, LITT. D.

Pastor of The Peoples Church, Toronto

MARSHALL, MORGAN & SCOTT, LTD.

LONDON :: EDINBURGH

MARSHALL, MORGAN AND SCOTT, LTD.
33 LUDGATE HILL,
LONDON, E.C.4

U.S.A.
VAN KAMPEN PRESS
222 EAST WILLOW STREET
WHEATON
ILLINOIS

CANADA
EVANGELICAL PUBLISHERS
366 BAY STREET
TORONTO

THE PEOPLES PRESS
100 BLOOR EAST
TORONTO

First Edition, 1932
Second Impression, 1934
Third Impression, 1937
Fourth Impression, 1939
Fifth Impression, 1943
Sixth Impression, 1945
Seventh Impression, 1946
Eighth Impression, 1948
Ninth Impression, 1950
Tenth Impression 1953

NOTE

MADE AND PRINTED IN GREAT BRITAIN BY PURNELL AND SONS, LTD.,
PAULTON (SOMERSET) AND LONDON

INTRODUCTION

D R. SMITH writes as he preaches. His book carries in its rhetoric the rhythm of the rambling brook. It states great, spiritual verities, without "mummifying" them. It is vibrant. It brings into expression, page after page, the pulsing heart throbs of its author. It bears a message that grips. Contrary to most theological treaties, this book is remarkably readable. There is nothing prosaic about it.

The "table of contents" bespeaks the burning issues that the book covers. Nothing is more needed in the Church to-day than a clear, concise and Scriptural plea for separation, Spirit-filling and service.

The Church has swung loose from its mooring at Immanuel's land, and has drifted far out into the sea of worldliness. *The Bible doctrine of Sanctification* may have been bandied about by eradicationists, but it bears a message that saints surely need. Sanctification is the will of God. There is no excuse for the Christian to live in subjection to either the world, the flesh, or the devil. Christ will lead the believing and the yielded soul into "the train of His triumph."

The blessed truths of the Spirit-filled life are open to all the saved.

The Holy Spirit came as the promise of the Father in answer to the needs of the Church.

The Spirit came to abide for the age. He indwells

every believer. He is God's "paraclete," sent to walk at the side of saints.

The Holy Spirit is the "element" into which the saints at Pentecost were baptized; all the saved since that day have been baptized in that One Spirit, into one Body.

The "filling" of the Spirit is the acme of Christian experience. "Be filled with the Spirit" is God's command to saints, not to sinners. The key to the Spirit-filled life is yieldedness. We "present," we yield; the Spirit takes control. He fills. A definite, and conscious filling with the Spirit results in a new and gracious manifestation of the choicest of divine graces in the daily walk.

Separation and Scriptural Sanctification both precede and follow the filling of the Spirit. They precede in the sense that the Spirit will fill only the life that is, in its purpose and desire, separated from the world, cleansed from conscious sinning and dedicated unto God. They follow the filling of the Spirit in the sense that the attitude of Separation and Spiritual Sanctification is potentially possible only after the Spirit has taken control.

Separation is vital to every normal Christian life. Saints were taken "out of the world," they are "not of the world" and if they live Godly they will be "hated by the world." The only place for a true disciple to dwell is outside the camp with his despised and rejected Lord.

The task of the Church—What is it? According to human speculation it is one thing; according to divine revelation it is quite another. The Church has no excuse for entering into schemes for social and civic betterment. The Church is set for the one by one method of evangelization through the

one and only message of the Evangel—Christ Jesus
crucified, risen and coming again.

Dr. Smith has done well to lend his heart and
pen in presenting these and other acid tests of
vitalized Christianity. He does not conceive of
Christianity as a creed to be memorized and carefully shelved for Sunday worship. He conceives
of Christianity as a Life created by and centred
in a person, the Lord Jesus Christ, and put to use
for that Person in a world steeped in sin but sought
by One mighty to save.

We commend the book and its message. It
should be read, and afterwards translated into
Christian life and service.

R. E. NEIGHBOUR.

Chicago, Ill.

Why should anyone hear the Gospel twice
before everyone has heard it once?

Oswald J. Smith

CONTENTS

Deeper and Deeper.

O. J. S.   OSWALD J. SMITH.

1. In - to the heart of Je - sus, deep-er and deep-er I go,
2. In - to the will of Je - sus, deep-er and deep-er I go,
3. In - to the cross of Je - sus, deep-er and deep-er I go,
4. In - to the joy of Je - sus, deep-er and deep-er I go,
5. In - to the love of Je - sus, deep-er and deep-er I go,

Seek-ing to know the rea - son why He should love me so—
Praying for grace to fol - low, seek-ing His way to know;
Fol - low-ing through the gar - den, fac - ing the dread - ed foe—
Ris - ing with soul en - rap - tured far from the world be - low;
Prais-ing the One who brought me out of my sin and woe;

Why He should stoop to lift me up from the mir - y clay,
Bow-ing in full sur - ren - der low at His bless - ed feet,
Drink-ing the cup of sor - row, sob-bing with brok - en heart;
Joy in the place of sor - row, peace in the midst of pain,
And through e - ter - nal a - ges grate-ful-ly I shall sing;

rall ....

Sav - ing my soul, making me whole, Though I had wandered a-way.
Bidding Him take, break me and make, Till I am moulded and meet.
"Oh, Sav-iour, help! dear Saviour, help! Grace for my weakness impart."
Je - sus will give, Je - sus will give, He will up-hold and sus - tain.
"Oh, how He loved! oh, how He loved! Je - sus! my Lord and my King."

THE MAN GOD USES

CHAPTER I

A BIRTHDAY PRAYER

ON November 8th, 1927, my thirty-eighth
birthday, I prayed this prayer: *"Lord, make
me a man after Thine own heart."* Work
faded out of sight; things that before seemed important disappeared; everything in which I was
interested took a secondary place, and my own
inner life before God was all that mattered, all
that was really worth while. And as I paced
back and forth in my study that day I prayed,
and prayed in the Spirit: *"Lord, make me a man
after Thine own heart."*

"I want, dear Lord, a heart that's true and clean—
　A sunlit heart with not a cloud between;
A heart like Thine, a heart divine, a heart as white as
　snow—
　On me, dear Lord, a heart like this bestow."

I saw as I had never seen before, that the big thing
was not the work I was doing, the books I was

writing, the sermons I was preaching, the crowds that gathered nor the success achieved; but rather the life I was living, the thoughts I was thinking, heart holiness, practical righteousness; in a word: my transformation, by the Spirit, into Christ-like-ness.

And there came to me with new and deeper meaning than ever before the words: *"Oh, for a closer walk with God !"* And my heart went out in a cry of anguish for such an experience. *"That I might know Him."* Thus prayed the great Apostle. *"Christ in you,"* he said again. And then, *"Christ liveth in me."* Yes, *"Noah walked with God;" "Enoch walked with God."* Could not I? Am not I more precious to God than my work, my possessions? God wanted me, not merely my service.

> " Take myself, and I will be
> Ever, only, ALL for Thee."

After that He led me out in prayer, a prayer that would make me *a man after His own heart*, and these were the petitions: "Lord, here are my hands; I consecrate them to Thee. May they never touch anything that Thou wouldst not have them touch, or do anything that would dishonour Thee. And here are my feet; I dedicate them to Thee. May they never go where Thou wouldst not be seen. Here, Lord, are my eyes. May they never look upon anything that would grieve Thy Holy Spirit. May my ears never listen to anything dishonouring to Thy name. May my mouth never be opened to speak a word that I would not want Thee to hear. May my mind never retain a thought nor an imagination that would dim the sense of Thy presence. May my heart know no love, and cherish no feeling that is not of Thee. Amen!"

> " Lord, I give my all to Thee,
>   Friends and time and earthly store,
> Soul and body, Thine to be,
>   Wholly Thine forever more."

And as I prayed there came to me these words: "I beseech you therefore, brethren, by the mercies of God, that ye present your bodies a living sacrifice, holy, acceptable unto God, which is your reasonable service. And be not conformed to this world; but be ye transformed, by the renewing of your mind, that ye may prove what is that good, and acceptable, and perfect will of God" (Rom. xii. 1-2). Then this: "Let not sin therefore reign in your mortal body, that ye should obey it in the lusts thereof. Neither yield ye your members as instruments of unrighteousness unto sin: but yield yourselves unto God. For sin shall not have dominion over you" (Rom. vi. 12-14).

God, I saw, demanded my *undivided attention*. Everything else must take a second place. Friends and loved ones, home, money, work—all, even though legitimate—all must give way to Christ. Day and night my *undivided attention* must be given to Him. God first! Such must be my attitude toward Him. Only then would He be able to bless and use me. Only thus could I satisfy His heart of love. For in my relationship to God I saw that none other and naught else must ever come between. That just as a husband comes first in the affections of his wife,

and vice-versa, so God must come first in my heart.
And just as no marriage can ever be a happy marriage where either husband or wife withhold their
undivided attention from each other, so my fellowship with God could only be complete when He had
my *undivided attention*. He would have me wait
on Him continually.

> " All for Jesus, all for Jesus!
>   All my being's ransomed powers;
>   All my thoughts, and words, and doings,
>   All my days and all my hours."

And what He asked of me that day He asks of
all alike. Can it be that we would deny Him His
right? Is there anything in this world worthy of that
attention He claims? Why, then, do we withhold
what He asks? Is true joy to be found outside of God?
Can we be happy with "things"? Do "things"
satisfy? "A man's life consisteth not in the abundance of the *things* which he possesseth" (Luke xii.
15). God has made us for Himself. He longs for our
fellowship and communion. To walk with Him
moment by moment, right here in the midst of a
wicked and perverse generation, in a world that
has no use for a separated, Holy Ghost life, a world
whose God is Satan—to walk with God as the sainted
Brainerd and the seraphic Fletcher walked when
they were here, to live as pilgrims and strangers
in a world that crucified our Lord—that is His
design and His purpose for us. How then can we
bear to disappoint Him, and thus fail to win His
approbation?

God wants us to be one hundred per cent for

Him. And so the question arises: Are we *out and out* for Jesus Christ? Are we *wholly God's*? Not ninety per cent, mark you, but one hundred per cent. Completely given over to God. Let us ask Him, then, to detach us from "things"; to detach us from the world, from our families and homes, from all that is meant by the "flesh"; to so wean us that we can give Him our *undivided attention*. There is much in the flesh that is legitimate. Can we deny ourselves even that which is legitimate for the Kingdom of Heaven's sake if our ministry should necessitate separation from our loved ones even for long periods at a time, in order that we may be *wholly God's*? And can we by His grace so rise above the world and the flesh in our detachment that we will find Jesus Himself, through His indwelling Spirit, sufficient to enable us to live *out and out* for Him, exclaiming from a heart filled with praise: "Jesus satisfies?" That is what He taught me, and that is what I mean when I talk of being *wholly God's, out and out* for Jesus Christ, one hundred per cent for Him, and thus becoming *a man after God's own heart*.

So, then, to be *a man after God's own heart* means to put God first; to walk with Him every moment; to do nothing that would displease Him and to allow nothing that would grieve Him; to live a life of practical righteousness and holiness before Him; to give Him our undivided attention, and to love Him supremely.

David, you remember, was *a man after God's own heart*. If David, after his failure, could be such a man, cannot I, cannot you? "Daniel purposed in his heart that he would not defile himself" (Dan.

i. 18). Let us "purpose," and God will give the enabling power.

For it is in this way that we become Christ-like; and that is God's highest ambition for us, viz., that we should be like His Son, transformed into the same image. To be a Christian for ten years and to be no more like Jesus then than at the time of conversion, is a tragedy. There are some who have only been saved six months who are more like Christ than others who have been on the way for six years. Only those who spend much time in His presence will ever become like Him. Only those who give Him their undivided attention will really come to know Him.

To get His best we must give Him our best. To become men and women after His heart we must let Him have our undivided attention. To win we must surrender. To live we must die. To receive we must give.

And, oh! the sweetness of such a life, the joy of His fellowship! There is nothing like it on earth. All the success in the world will not compensate for it. He is "the Lily of the Valley," "the Bright and Morning Star," "the Rose of Sharon," "the Chiefest among Ten Thousand," "the One Altogether lovely." Friends can never mean so much. Even loved ones disappoint. Money brings its burdens, and fame its bitterness. But He, He satisfies. God is never a disappointment. To walk with Him is the sweetest thing on earth. To know that all is well, that there is nothing between, that no black cloud of sin hides His face—ah! that is Heaven indeed.

Oh the joy of full surrender!
  How it thrills me through and through!
Every talent for my Saviour,
  While I seek His will to do.

Then let us pray it, mean it and live it: *"Lord make me a man after Thine own heart."*

CHAPTER II

THE MAN GOD USES

I HAVE been trying to think during these past days of the qualities that will enable God to use men in Christian service; and so far as I can discover there are at least eight that are essential. Moreover, I am absolutely convinced that any man who is willing to pay the price may be used of God regardless of talents and gifts, not perhaps to the extent of some, but certainly to the full limit of his capacity, and if not the fault is his.

Now, it may cost a good deal. God does not always reveal the whole price at once. But when we reach the place where we are so desperately in earnest about it that we are willing to make any sacrifice, then it is that God can begin to use us.

Well do I remember how I walked up and down my room in prayer exclaiming: "Oh, God, use me, use me, no matter what the cost! Gladly will I pay any price if only I may be used of Thee." Are you willing to pay the price?

1. *The man God uses is the man who has but one great purpose in life.*

A divided heart can never bring complete satisfaction. The man of mingled interests will seldom

8

make a success of anything. If he would succeed in business he must give the major portion of his time and the best of his thought to his business. It is the man who divides his time between the office and the gambling table who fails. If his affections are divided between his wife and another woman married life is bound to end in disaster. Nor could any young man be satisfied unless he held the supreme place in the heart of the woman whom he would make his wife.

The very same is true of the man who would be used of God, only to a far greater degree. The work alone must claim his whole attention. He has no room for other things. Paul was a man of "one thing." "This one thing I do," he exclaimed. That was the secret of his success. He had a great surging passion to make known the Gospel, and he gave himself day and night to his work. And in writing to Timothy, he commanded, "be diligent in these things; give thyself wholly to them."

The trouble is that men are interested in too many things to-day to be used of God. I have known college students whose interests were so divided between their studies and girl friends that their lives made no impression whatever. And let me say that no young man can be mightily used of God who is continually spending his evenings, his time and thought in the society of women.

I know of ministers who are in business on the side. Their whole time is not given to their one great work. Before I entered the ministry I purchased a vacant lot for speculative purposes, but after my ordination I sold it as quickly as possible that I might be perfectly free to give my whole thought to my work.

I am not urging that you have no other interests in life. There are duties to which you are bound to give your attention. What I do insist upon is that you make them as few as possible, and above all that you consider them as secondary, thus putting God and His work first and looking upon it as your one great purpose in life.

2. *The man God uses is the man who by God's grace has removed every hindrance from his life.*

Now then, you don't need to tell me what it is that hinders God from using you. God knows and you know. You must get right with Him. It may be only a weight or it may be a definite sin, possibly your besetting sin. Perhaps it is impurity in thought, word or deed. Possibly it is pride, jealousy, malice, covetousness, unbelief, or self in one form or another. It may be tobacco. But whatever it is it must be removed before God can use you. Remember, it was Achan who caused Israel to fail. Is there an Achan in your heart, a shelf behind the door, a sin that no one sees but God? People think you are what you appear to be; but do they really know you as you are? Dare you withdraw the veil and let them see all? (Isa. lix. 1–2).

3. *The man God uses is the man who has placed himself absolutely at God's disposal.*

Some of us act as though we were afraid of God, afraid to let Him have full sway. God says, "If any man willeth to do His will." What could the potter do if the clay refused to yield? What could

the doctor do if the patient refused to trust? Of
what value are insubordinate soldiers? "He that
walketh in a perfect way, he shall serve me"
(Ps. ci. 6).

Well, then, are you yielded? Have you said an
eternal "Yes" to God and an eternal "No" to self?
Are you dedicated? Have you surrendered all? Has
your will been set aside, and have you accepted
His for your life? Will you go where He wants
you to go, and be what He wants you to be? Are
you able to sing every verse of Frances Ridley
Havergal's great consecration hymn, "Take my
life"? Do you mean it? And can you say with all
your heart:

> " Lord, I give myself to Thee,
>   Friends and time and earthly store;
>   Soul and body Thine to be—
>   Wholly Thine for evermore."

4. *The man God uses is the man who has learned
how to prevail in prayer.*

The men who have been greatly used of God
have all been mighty in prayer. As you read their
biographies you discover that the spirit of prayer
predominates. Jacob exclaims: "I will not let
Thee go except Thou bless me," and hears God say:
"Thou hast striven with God and with men and
hast prevailed." Jesus in the midst of the greatest
activity and opportunity for service withdraws from
the multitude and seeks a solitary place in which to
pray, sometimes spending whole nights alone with
His Father, praying with such anguish of spirit
that His sweat turns to blood. And this is the story

of every man who has been used of God. Are you willing to pay the price?

You may be marvellously gifted and equipped for the service of God, but if you have not learned how to prevail in prayer you can never expect God's blessing on your labours. Let me urge upon each one the necessity of withdrawing to the secret place to pray the prevailing prayer, the prayer that effects its object. We must pray through and get the answer. Oh, for a return to the prayer-life of such men as Bramwell, Ostoby, Carvasso, John Smith and Finney!

5. *The man God uses is the man who is a student of the Word.*

God's Word is your weapon. If you doubt its strength what power can you have in wielding it? It is your only source of information. When the Word of God becomes your meat and drink, your daily study and a very part of yourself, then, and not until then, will you be able to use it as He intends. Do you believe that the text you proclaim is the living, inspired Word of God? And are you confident that it will never return void? God cannot use a man who doubts His word.

6. *The man God uses is the man who has a vital, living message for a lost world.*

You are looking forward to the foreign field. Well, what are you going to tell them? Have you a message? Why are you going?

If your mission is merely one of Social Service, Education, Political Reform, you had better leave it to the social service expert, the school teacher, the doctor and the reformer. If it is to substitute Western civilization along with the Christian religion for heathenism, better leave it to government agencies with their systems of uplift and reform.

Ah no! there is only one message great enough to take us from our homes of comfort, carry us across the seas, and set us down in the midst of persecution, ridicule, sacrifice and loneliness, and that is the message that "Christ died for our sins," the message that "God so loved the world that He gave His only begotten Son, that whosoever believeth in Him should not perish but have everlasting life," the message of the Cross. Nothing less will suffice. "Go ye and preach the Gospel." The rest is the business of the state.

But what message have you for the homeland? Why are you entering the ministry? If it is merely to entertain you had better turn your work over to the theatres for they can do it better than you can. If it is to educate the people by reading religious essays, better advise them to study Carlyle, Emerson, Browning and Shakespeare. It will cut down expenses and save them the necessity of coming out in bad weather. Besides they can cultivate a taste for poetry in clubs held for that purpose. Or if it is simply to charm them by the beauty of oratory or great musical compositions, the chautauqua and concert hall will answer better.

Oh, my brother, you have a far greater work than this. The highest, most glorious, and most important of all callings is yours. The others have their individual vocations but yours embraces all, for you deal with all classes and conditions. Nor have you any time for argument or controversy. Yours is a Message that God has commissioned you to deliver, a Message of life and death, and He will hold you responsible for your stewardship. Oh, that you might realize the greatness of your task!

We are not in the pulpit to please and entertain, nor are we to parade ourselves. "The minstrel who sings before you to show his skill will be praised for his wit, rhymes and voice, but the courier, who hurries to bring you a message, will be forgotten in the message that he brings." Oh, my brethren, what do men think of us? Do they say: "What a great sermon!" or "What a great Christ! What a wonderful saviour!"

Remember, we are to represent Jesus, and that means that we must be dead in earnest, for to some our message will mean death, to others life. Then let us preach as though we mean what we say. A great actor one time explained the difference between actors and ministers by saying: "You clergymen talk about real things as though they were unreal, while we actors talk about unreal things as though they were real."

Listen, my friend: If you are firmly convinced that "all have sinned," that men are lost, and that Jesus Christ is the only One who can save them, and you go forth to proclaim that message, then I bid you God-speed; and let me tell you, your ministry will be glorious.

Oh, then, let me ask you again: Have you a message that the Holy Spirit honours? Does He convict of sin when you preach? Are souls saved and believers edified? Are you proclaiming man-made sermons or God-given messages? For if your message is born of the Holy Ghost you need never be ashamed. Thousands have flocked to hear it all down the centuries, and thousands will do the same again. Audiences have been held spellbound by the simple Gospel Message, and it still grips. No need to fear. Go forth then and speak, confident of His power.

7. *The man God uses is the man of Faith, who expects results.*

The great trouble with the majority of us is that we do not expect anything to happen. We are not looking for results. We are content to go on in the same old hum-drum way, and if a soul in anguish should cry out: "What must I do to be saved?" we should be dumbfounded.

I have never yet been content to see things go on in the usual quiet way. Unless something happened I felt I had failed. I have always expected the extraordinary, nor have I been disappointed.

You remember that young preacher who came to Mr. Spurgeon discouraged because he was not seeing results.

"Why, you don't mean to tell me," exclaimed Spurgeon, "that you expect results every time *you* preach, do you?"

"Well, no," responded the young man, somewhat taken back.

"Then that is why you don't get them," was the pointed reply.

I notice that when men play football they do not kick the ball at random, but they endeavour to drive it into the goal, and so with hockey. And, thank God, we too can have a goal.

I never saw a race where men ran this way and that, all over the field. They had an object in view, and they ran toward a certain point. And we too are in a race, but a race, thank God, for souls.

When a lawyer pleads a case he does not merely entertain. He is there for a verdict. And, praise God, we are out for a verdict. Nor should we be satisfied without one.

In a shooting match every man fires at a mark. Have we a mark, and do we take aim?

In the days of the Great War recruiting meetings were held, not to entertain, but to secure recruits. Apart from this result the meeting was in vain. Are we looking for recruits for our King, and do we expect some to respond? Let us have faith for definite results.

8. *The man God uses is the man who works in the Anointing of the Holy Spirit.*

"Tarry ye in the city of Jerusalem, until ye be endued with power from on High." They tarried. "Ye shall receive power, after that the Holy Ghost is come upon you : and ye shall be witnesses unto me." And the thought of witnessing without that power never entered their minds.

Read the biographies of God's men and you will discover that each one sought and obtained the Enduement of Power from on High. One sermon preached in the Anointing is worth a thousand in the energy of the flesh.

This, then, is the man God uses. He has but one purpose in life. Every hindrance has been removed.

He places himself absolutely at God's disposal. He has learned how to prevail in prayer. He is a student of the Word. He has a vital, living Message for a lost world. He expects results. And he works in the Anointing of the Holy Spirit. Oh, my brethren, let us see to it that we have these eight qualifications in order that God may use us to the fullest possible extent. Then will our Ministry be glorious indeed.

CHAPTER III

THE SEPARATED LIFE

IT is doubtful if there ever was a time when the note of Separation needed to be sounded more than to-day. The world has become so churchy and the Church so worldly that it is hard to distinguish the one from the other. The line of demarcation has been so completely broken down that churches, where revivals once flourished, whose spiritual life was at one time deep and strong, are to-day mere social centres over which God has long ago written the word "Ichabod"—"The glory has departed."

But worldliness in the professing church is only another sign of the end of the age. The prophetic utterances of God's Word are being literally fulfilled. It cannot be long now before He comes.

People seem to have the idea that we must mingle with the world and become like it in order to win souls and influence lives for God. Yet when a man falls into a deep well no one ever dreams of jumping down alongside of him in order to get him out. Instead he stays away up at the top and from there lets down a ladder or rope and thus lifts him up.

Ah, no! The men who have won souls and influenced other lives for God have been the men who

have walked with God far above the masses, and
thus from an altitude of spirituality have drawn
others up to their level. The only way to win others
is to be different ourselves and thus attract by something they lack, and by prevailing with God prevail
with men.

Had Abraham gone to live with Lot in Sodom
his influence would have availed but little. It was
when he separated himself and stood afar off on the
highlands of faith with God that his intercessions
secured Lot's deliverance. Let us be separate. We
must dwell apart with God.

Then I want to say that the world expects the
Christian to be different. It has its own standard
of what a saint should be. And even when it suc-
ceeds in drawing us down to its level it but mocks
and laughs at our plight. No longer does it respect
us nor reverence our position. We are then no
better than others.

A young woman who saw no harm in dancing
decided to do some personal work during the dance,
and while gliding over the floor with her companion,
she suddenly turned and asked him if he was a
Christian.

"A Christian! No! Why, are you?" he exclaimed
in amazement.

"Yes," replied the young woman. "I'm a
Christian."

"Well, then, for God's sake, why are you here?"
was the unexpected response.

Ah yes, the world expects the Christian to be
different. Otherwise how will anyone know which
is which? If there is no line of demarcation how
will people know which side we are on? If we
dress and act like the world how can anyone tell

whether we are Christians or not? There must be a difference.

Now, separation has always been God's standard. Abraham had to leave his country, and his father's home and in complete separation, go he knew not whither. Moses refused to be called the son of Pharaoh's daughter, choosing rather to suffer affliction with the people of God, than to enjoy the pleasures of sin for a season; esteeming the reproach of Christ greater riches than the treasures in Egypt. So also with the Israelites. They were a peculiar people, entirely separated from the nations around about them, representing God. And in Ezra ix. 10 and Neh. xiii. when the line of separation had been broken down by mixed marriages there was no leniency shown. Heathen wives must be put away and separation of the severest character again instituted.

Yes, and separation is still the call of God. "Come out from among them, and be ye separate, saith the Lord," and, "Be ye not unequally yoked together with unbelievers" (2 Cor. vi. 14–18). The world must be forsaken and separation maintained.

Let us remember our character. According to God's Word we are "pilgrims and strangers," "sojourners," a heavenly people in a foreign country. This is not our home.

> I'm but a pilgrim here,
>   A stranger from afar;
> And to my distant home
>   With many a battle scar,
> My Lord will bear me safe at last
> When pilgrim days on earth are past.

Enmity and hatred is the attitude of the world toward the true child of God. "If ye were of the world, the world would love his own: but because ye are not of the world, therefore the world hateth you" (Jn. xv. 19). What about it? Does the world hate you? If you are not of it, if you do not belong to it, and if you make it clear that you are a pilgrim and a stranger, then you will very quickly discover that the world hates you. You see it depends on the attitude you take toward it.

Now, the evidence of the separated life lies in the attitude of the heart, not the actions, towards the world. "Love not the world, neither the things that are in the world. If any man love the world, the love of the Father is not in him" (1 Jn. ii. 15). Hence, it is not necessary to actually take part in the things of the world. The real question is: Do you want to? Is there a desire? Does the world appeal and allure? If so, then there is no heart separation after all.

Listen again: "Ye adulterers and adulteresses, know ye not that the friendship of the world is enmity with God? Whosoever therefore will be a friend of the world is the enemy of God" (Jas. iv. 4). Pretty plain language! Talk about a "worldly Christian!" God declares that the world's friend is His enemy. The one who loves the world does not love God. What then is my heart attitude? That is the important question, Do I love the world or do I love God? Am I the world's friend or God's friend? Would the word "adulterer" or "adulteress" be applicable to me? What is the real attitude of my heart toward the world? Not my actions but my thoughts, my likes and dislikes.

Suppose a woman were to live with her husband

on Sunday, and then spend her time with other men during the rest of the week, and on Sunday return again to her husband, what would we think of her? What would we call her? How long would her husband acquiesce? And yet that is how the so-called "worldly Christian" treats the Lord Jesus Christ. Six days in the world and then one day with Christ. No wonder such an one is called an "adulterer" or an "adulteress" in Jas. iv. 4. What a disgraceful life to live! Companionship with the enemies of God! Such conduct is viewed by God as "unfaithfulness." The worldly Christian in His sight is likened to an unfaithful wife. Must the child of God be compared to a harlot? Yet such is the description in the inspired Word. Let us ponder very carefully 1 Jn. ii. 15 and Jas. iv. 4. The Old Testament, especially in the prophets, is full of such comparisons. Separation is the only remedy.

Now, the separated life means separation from:

1. *Worldly Pleasures.*

That was the choice Moses made when he repudiated the pleasures of sin (Heb. xi. 24-26). The dance, the theatre, and the card party are not of God, but of the world. They were introduced not by spiritual leaders and saintly men, but by men of the world. The spirit of the world pervades such pleasures, and prayer and testimony in the midst of these things is out of the question. The two simply don't go together. The people who throng such gatherings do not attend nor take part in prayer meetings, nor are they interested in the spiritual work of the Church. Hence, the time must come when the true Christian is willing to obey the clear and emphatic command: "Come out from among them, and be ye separate," and to sing from the heart:

> Goodbye, Old World, goodbye!
>   I want no more of thee,
> For God is dearer far than thou canst ever be;
>   My soul is satisfied
>   With Christ the Crucified;
> And all I need I find in Him alone.

2. *Worldly Alliances.*

"Be ye not unequally yoked together with unbelievers." No words could be clearer, no command more emphatic. God cannot honour the unequal yoke.

(1) Business Alliances.

The Christian who enters into partnership with an unbeliever or even with a so-called worldly Christian is running a dangerous risk. Pray as he will he has no promise of blessing in God's Word. No wonder so many business enterprises fail. To disobey the plain Word of Scripture is to invite disaster. How can God bless what he has condemned?

(2) Lodge Alliances.

Secret societies are the curse of the Church everywhere. The lodge may be good enough for the man

B

of the world, but for God's child the Church of Jesus Christ should more than suffice.

In the secret societies are to be found Jews and Unitarians, men who deny the deity of Jesus Christ. Even the name of the Lord Jesus is not permitted for fear of giving offence. And I want to say that the place that is not good enough for my Lord is not good enough for me. Nor could I go in when He is kept out.

Oh, how clearly God has spoken! "Be not un-equally yoked together with unbelievers." Is a Jew an unbeliever? Are Unitarians unbelievers? Most certainly. Then, thus saith the Lord: "Come out from among them, and be ye separate." God help us to obey.

But you say, "once a Mason always a Mason." Oh no! Not a bit of it. That is a man-made law, and it has never been sanctioned by God. No, my brother, you can cut clean, renounce the whole thing, break every satanic vow you ever took before your eyes were open, and step out into the clear light of God's Word, separated for ever from every secret abomination.

(3) Marriage Alliances.

Oh, how many have admitted that the secret of all their unhappiness in married life lay in the fact that they disobeyed God and took on the unequal yoke. God's Word here also is very, very plain. "She is at liberty to be married to whom she will; *only in the Lord*" (1 Cor. vii. 39). "Only in the Lord." And to marry one who is not in the Lord is to court disappointment. How can God's blessing rest on the home when His Word has been violated?

Many a young woman has had to face this problem and break her engagement; whilst others who have persisted in disobeying have lived to regret it beyond words to express. Nor does the plea that it is her purpose to marry, in order to win, avail in the least. The girl who fails to win her future husband for Christ before marriage has but little hope of winning him after.

Oh, Christian worker, don't, don't for your own sake, disobey the Word of God and enter the unequal yoke! It may seem hard now, but be certain of this: God has another and a far better plan for your life. To ignore His Word is dangerous. To obey it is always safe. There need be no question as to the results. Therefore, "Be ye not unequally yoked together with unbelievers."

3. *Worldly Companions.*

Here again there must be a breaking away. Worldly companions will not enjoy the Christians' prayer meeting, nor can the child of God take pleasure in their pursuits. Sooner or later the spirit of their association will dull spiritually unless a complete separation takes place. It is difficult to play with fire and not be burned.

But you say: How can I give them up? Child of God, you will not have to give them up. You live a spiritual life and they will very soon give *you* up. They will be as uncomfortable in your presence as you will be when with them.

Make friends of God's children. And whether they be brown or yellow, black or white, you will find them far more precious and the association closer and more binding than even that of blood relations out of Christ. They will understand when the members of your own family do not. And then, too, such friendships can never be broken. Death does not separate. Make friends, therefore, of those with whom you can associate not only here but throughout Eternity.

Now, the secret of the separated life lies in "the expulsive power of a new affection." I will never forget the day Grace Armstrong was converted. It was at a Sunday afternoon meeting in Chicago. She just slid down on her knees and sobbed as though her heart would break. No one could console her. Then as she went out her girl friends told her that it would soon pass away.

"No, girls," responded Grace, "this never will pass away."

And when young men telephoned her and invited her to the theatre, without a moment's hesitation she answered, "No." Old things had passed away in a single moment. No longer did she love the pleasures of the world. All things had become new. Christ was now in her heart and she had a new affection. She loved the prayer meeting, loved to stand and sing for her Saviour on the street corner, loved to do personal work, loved above everything else the House of God. There were no battles, no questions to answer, no problems to solve. When Christ came in in His glorious fulness the world went out. There was no room for it. Grace is now with her Lord, but oh, what a wonderful testimony she left before she went home!

When I was a missionary among the Indians near Alaska, I lived for some time on what we called "hardtack." "Dog biscuit" I suppose would be the name in civilization. Now, it was hard, so hard

that only by warming it could I manage to pene-
trate it with my teeth. Nevertheless I thoroughly
enjoyed and relished it.

But there came a day when I returned to civilization, and began to eat bread and butter once more.
And, what do you think? Why, I have never
wanted hardtack since. Not once have I pined for
the old days and cried, "Oh, for a bit of hardtack
once more!" And why? Simply because I've
found something better.

Well, you can have the hardtack if you want it;
but as for me, I am going to feast on bread and
butter. I want the best. And, thank God, when
we enter into the spiritual experiences of the New
Birth and the Holy Ghost, we are fully satisfied;
nor do we crave any more for the things of the
world. Thus separation becomes easy. It is not
hard to deny yourself something that you do not
want. Thus, it is "the expulsive power of a new
affection." Let Jesus Christ in in all His fulness,
open your heart to the Holy Spirit, become God-
inhabited, and you will be glad to go without the
camp with Him bearing His reproach.

" Since mine eyes were fixed on Jesus
        I've lost sight of all beside,
    So enchained my spirit's vision
        Looking at the Crucified."

CHAPTER IV

THE SUPREME TEST

"LOVEST thou Me?"

The question was startling. The little group, sitting round the fire on the shore of the Galilean sea, glanced quickly up at the speaker's face. With expectation gleaming in His eyes, He sat quietly gazing at but one, and waiting for the answer.

The early dawn was gently stealing over the hills far away in the distance, ushering in a new day and chasing away the darkness of the night. Save for the rumbling of the waves along the shore, and the occasional cry of some lonely sea-bird, no sound broke the quiet stillness of the early morn.

All through the long dreary night they had toiled with their nets and taken nothing. Then as the dawn began to break, a figure, strange, mysterious, stood upon the shore. Discouragement and weariness gave way to fear. With straining eyes they sought to pierce the rising mist, but all in vain, till suddenly, the youngest of them recognized the silent, ghost-like form and cried:

"It is the Lord!"

Like a flash, Peter—poor, remorseful Peter, his great heart yearning with an almost superhuman

28

devotion—leaps into the water, and with strong powerful strokes, soon reaches the shore. The others follow. The net is drawn in. A fire of coals is burning, and fish are cooking. Not a word is spoken until the Master, Himself, gives the simple invitation:

"Come and dine."

Quietly the food is eaten. All is still. Awe and reverence makes speech impossible. Finally, Jesus again breaks the silence with the words of our text:

"Lovest thou Me?"

It is Peter to whom He is speaking, great, blundering Peter; the disciple who so recently denied Him, who "went out and wept bitterly." He would test him. Peter must make a triple confession of his devotion for his threefold denial. He would try him by the highest possible standard, the "Supreme Test."

"Simon, son of Jonas, esteemest thou Me?"

He is pleading for that higher love, the love of the intellect or will, rather than the human emotion. But Peter is no longer sure of himself. He failed once; he may fail again. And so, unwilling to make the higher profession implied in his Master's question, he uses the word expressing mere emotional love or personal attachment:

"Yea, Lord, Thou knowest that I love Thee."

Again, the question is asked. The response is the same. Then the Master accepts Peter's own word, seeing that Peter will not rise to His, and for the third time asks:

"Simon, son of Jonas, lovest thou Me?"

And Peter, great noble Peter, his heart almost bursting with grief to think that his Lord should doubt him, replied with throbbing pulse and quivering voice:

"Lord, Thou knowest all things, Thou knowest that I love Thee!"

"Dost thou love Me?" With emotion
Comes the answer of devotion:
"Lord, Thou knowest that I love Thee."
"Feed My sheep," He answers, softly.

"Peter, Peter, dost thou love Me
More than these and all around thee?"
"Lord, Thou knowest naught can sever,
And that I am Thine forever."

Silence reigning, moments fleeting,
Then the heart of love entreating:
"Peter, dost thou love Me?" "Master!"
And the breath comes thicker, faster.

"Master! Master!" sobbing, sobbing—
"Oh, Thou knowest!" throbbing, throbbing;
Pleads the great heart with emotion,
Bound to Christ by love's devotion.

And we have called this question the "Supreme Test." But was it after all the highest test of devotion and loyalty, the most binding avowal that human lips could utter? Was there not a greater? Did Jesus make a mistake? The life of Peter does not seem to indicate any such mistake. Jesus didn't seem to think so. In fact, He was willing to base all on that one simple question. He knew what He was doing, knew that He was asking the most vital question in all language. And to-day, after the lapse of nearly nineteen centuries, we may still look upon this question as the Supreme Test of our spiritual life.

There are three things I would have you note in which "Lovest thou Me?" becomes the Supreme Test. And the first of these is that it is

THE SUPREME TEST OF DISCIPLESHIP

Day by day, all down the centuries, Jesus Christ has been binding men and women to Himself. Not by force, not by fear, but by love. Satan was quite willing that He should have the kingdoms of the world providing He recognize His allegiance to him. But Jesus knew that it was not the Father's will to force men to obey Him. Ah, no! He would draw, not compel, win, not drive; men should choose Him of their own accord; they should be won by love. Such a union would be far closer, far stronger, and more lasting than forced obedience could ever be. Love had brought Him to earth; love had caused Him to die for a lost race, and love would draw men and women to Him. Could any oath of allegiance be stronger than the simple test He chose to put—"Lovest thou Me?"

Not a word does He ask regarding any one of a hundred questions that would naturally arise in the mind. Doctrine, dogma, creed, theology—not a word. Sin, repentance, service—not a syllable. One question only is asked. And mark you, it is His last chance. He is soon to leave. This is the best opportunity He would have for parting instructions and warnings. Has he no other word; are there no further conditions of discipleship; is there no creed or church formula to accept? No, none. And why? Because "Lovest thou Me?" includes and embraces all. The others will follow in their own places. The primary question will suffice for all else. "Lovest thou Me?" will lead on to all that is needful.

Thousands, to-day, are active church-members, splendid workers, but they have no personal love for Jesus Christ. Form and ceremony can never suffice. To be true to the great fundamentals of the Faith does not prove that you are true in heart to Jesus. Multitudes who are right in their heads are wrong in their hearts. Brethren, I would rather be right in heart and wrong in head than right in head and wrong in heart. It is because of this that there is so much controversy and hard feeling to-day. The lamentable fact of fundamentalism is its hardness and bitterness of spirit. God gave us a sickle, but not to use on our brethren. It is even possible to be a martyr for the Faith and yet not love Jesus Christ. Paul must have foreseen this when he wrote: "Though I give my body to be burned, and have not love, it profiteth me nothing."

You will recall the declaration of Jesus Himself regarding the first and greatest commandment which, with the second, embraces the entire law, "Thou shalt love the Lord thy God with all thy heart, and with all thy soul, and with all thy mind."

Oh, my brethren, we may not understand the great theological positions of our faith, yea, we may be ignorant of our own church dogmas, but if we sincerely love Jesus Christ we will have fulfilled all the law. It is the heart that must be right, and given a loving heart, a heart that yearns to please and follow Him, all else is certain.

But further: not only is it the Supreme Test of discipleship: it is also

THE SUPREME TEST OF CONDUCT

No longer do we find it necessary to ask the old question regarding our attitude toward worldly things: "Is it wrong to do this?" "Is it a sin to do that?" We simply apply the "Supreme Test" to all our actions. It becomes "the expulsive power of a new affection." It is not a case of whether it is right or wrong to indulge in questionable amusements. A man becomes so filled with the Spirit of God, so permeated with the love of Christ, and so anxious to serve and please the One who has won his heart's affections, that there is no room for sin, no room for the world, and he will have absolutely no desire for the things in which the unsaved delight. Think you a man would injure one whom he really loved? Nay, verily! Hence, the one great question, the "Supreme Test" of all, is love.

Oh, my brother, tell me, do you love Him, *do you love Him?* If so, you will want to please Him. If so, you will want to follow Him. If so, you will be fully satisfied with Him, Him and Him alone. The world will no longer draw. Its charms will cease to exist so far as you are concerned, and you will no more crave its empty pleasures. Jesus, Jesus, Himself, will be your all and in all. You will feed upon Him, dwell with Him, abide in Him, love Him, and crown Him as king of your heart. All your questions will be easily settled if you really love Him.

> " Thou, O Christ, art all I want ;
> More than all in Thee I find."

And in the last place, "Lovest thou Me?" is

THE SUPREME TEST OF SERVICE

In other words, it is the incentive of "love" rather than that of "duty." The follower of the Lord Jesus Christ serves his Master because he loves Him, and not because of any obligation he may wish to discharge.

What was it that drove David Brainerd to the savage Indians of the great, howling wilderness? What was it that made him leave his home at twenty-four years of age, and dwell alone in the heart of the wild, trackless forests of the interior; that enabled him though dying with consumption, weak and feeble from lack of food, long tiring rides on horseback, dismal, comfortless nights in the open woods under a pouring rain, to still press on month after month in order to tell his beloved Indians that God loved them, loved them to the extent that He gave His Son, His only Son, to die for them? What, I ask? Duty? Away with such a thought! No man would feel it his duty to do so much. No! No! It was "love." David Brainerd loved his Lord, and wanted to show it.

So with Judson, Livingstone, Morrison, Taylor, Carey, and all the great, heroic missionaries of the past. Yes, my brethren, and even so will it be with you, if you really love Him. You will prove it by glad, happy service. You will even lay down your life if need be—that is, if you love Him. Do you?

Oh, the breadth and length, the height and depth of His own great heart of infinite love and compassion! Love demands love. And nothing will satisfy a heart that loves except love. And so, because He Himself loves so greatly, He can be satisfied with nothing less that the love of His followers. What are wealth, houses, lands, luxury, and all that money can bestow to one who yearns for love? Love, and love only is the ground of acceptance with Christ. Hence, "Lovest thou Me?" becomes the "Supreme Test" for every Christian.

In one of the larger cities of France where Mrs. Booth Clibborn had been holding evangelistic meetings, she was one day visited by the wife of a very wealthy Frenchman. In her hand she held a small bottle marked "poison." In her heart was the calm determination to take her own life. She was only one of the hundreds of that sad and Godless country who go down to a suicide's grave. Before committing the deed, however, she made up her mind to see the only one in all France whom she felt she could trust, and look upon her face as she passed away. Let her own words tell the story:

"It was just the other day that I complained to my husband. Surprised and irritated, he replied:

"'Why, whatever do you want? You have my pocket-book; you have my home; you eat at my table. All that wealth and position can give are yours, and yet you complain.'

"'I want your heart,' I replied, 'I want you to love me.'

"'Oh!' he exclaimed, ' you can't have that. That belongs to another. You may have everything else, but my heart, my love—that is impossible.'"

And we may offer Jesus Christ everything else that we have, and still He will be unsatisfied. Love demands love. Nothing less can be sufficient And now in the same tender, pleading tones, and the same yearning heart, He comes to you and to me, and once again we hear Him ask the question that constitutes the "Supreme Test," and demands an answer, "Lovest thou Me?"

But you answer, "I do love Jesus." You do! Then what? "Feed my sheep." Prove it. Love is service. You had a splendid Prophetic Conference. You were fed. Now what? Is that all? Does it end there? Then your Conference has fallen short, far short. What about the "other sheep"? Have you no outlet? Has a lost world no claim on your love? That is why I am so tired of the average Bible Conference. It gets nowhere, and the stream becomes a stagnant pool for want of an outlet. And that is why I enjoy the Conferences and Conventions of great Missionary Movements. They end up with a spiritual torrent that flows out to all the world and produces life everywhere. Lives and money are laid on the altar. The people are given a chance to prove their love by sacrificial giving for the Regions Beyond.

If Jesus Christ should appear in our midst just now and personally put this question, "Lovest thou me?" to each one of us individually, what would we say? How would we answer Him? How searching it would be? Would we endeavour to avoid Him? Or are we in love with Jesus Christ? "We love Him," declared John. Do you? Do I?

CHAPTER V

THE VICTORIOUS LIFE

THE saddest thing in the life of many a Christian is the presence and power of sin. There are those who would gladly give all they possess if only they could resist temptation and live a life of unbroken fellowship with God.

It is a painful but familiar fact that there are thousands of men and women the world over who know Jesus Christ as their Saviour, but who have never experienced anything beyond conversion. Christ is not the supreme passion of their lives. Their experience is one of victory and defeat; to-day on the mountain top, to-morrow in the valley; the wilderness journey instead of Canaan's rest; the seventh chapter of Romans instead of the eighth.

When everything goes right, and nothing arises to interrupt the harmony of their lives, their victory is perfect; but when things go wrong, and they are upset in their plans, when provocation and opposition cross their pathway, when dark and foreboding clouds hover on their horizon, when trouble and adversity surround them, then their victory takes wings and flies away.

But there is a life, praise God, so far above the ordinary that it can only be compared to the brilliancy of the noonday sun in contrast to the

light of the evening star. It is beyond the fondest
hopes and dreams of multitudes of dissatisfied and
disappointed Christians.

And yet it is possible for all. Yea, more! it is
God's will for every child of His. "Sin shall not
have dominion" (Rom. iii. 14), declares the
inspired Word. And when Paul cried out, "O
wretched man that I am! who shall deliver me?"
he is able to answer with absolute assurance: "I
thank God . . . Jesus Christ our Lord" (Rom.
vii. 24–25).

And, oh, what a joy it is to be free! to have the
fetters snapped, the power of sin broken! That old
besetting habit that held me in bondage so long, that
unholy desire that conquered me again and again—
what a joy it is to know that the chains are gone!
Oh, yes, I tried, tried time after time to free myself.
Vows were taken and resolutions made, but all in
vain. I was chained and shackled until there
seemed to be no hope of freedom. Sinning and
repenting, praying and failing, weeping and indulg-
ing again. This was my experience. Oh, the
bitterness of sin.

But at last, at last, praise God, I was free; as
free as the Israelitish slaves when they stood
on the other shore and watched their enemies
perish beneath the waves. How my soul rejoiced!
What peace was mine! Oh, the heart-rest that
followed! Free, free at last! "I thank God through
Jesus Christ our Lord." Hallelujah! What a
Saviour!

There are two classes of sins that men are guilty
of committing. First, there are what might be
designated "Outward Sins"; and, second, "Inward
Sins."

Perhaps if we were to ask ourselves some very personal questions, it might help. We are not now referring to the first class; namely, Outward Sins, such as murder, theft, adultery, etc.; for if we are Christians at all, we are no longer guilty of these: but those sins which unseen by the eye of man rob us of the victory which Christ purchased for us, and are the cause of all our unhappiness and defeat.

1. *Have I been delivered from worry and anxiety?*

Now, worry is sin. "In nothing be anxious" (Phil. iv. 6, R.V.). and "Be not anxious for your life" (Matt. vi. 25–34, R.V.). Hence, to worry is to break the definite command of God. Moreover, worry shows a lack of trust. As some one has said, "Worry is a useless burden weighted with distrust of God." Jesus never worried. His life was calm, serene and trustful under all circumstances. Even amid the raging storm He could remain "asleep on a pillow."

2. *Have I been delivered from discouragement and despondency?*

Discouragement! That was the sin of Elijah. It is Satan's most formidable weapon, and it was frequently used on the Israelites during their wilderness journey. Then, too, there are despondent Christians, Christians who have lost their joy, confidence, cheerfulness and hope. Jesus was never discouraged nor despondent.

3. *Have I been delivered from irritation and discontent ?*

Do little things irritate and annoy? Am I dissatisfied? Do I murmur at my lot? (Philippians iv. 11). This was the besetting sin of the wilderness journey. Jesus never showed the least sign of irritation or discontent.

4. *Have I been delivered from anger and malice ?*

Is there any malice, spite, hatred or enmity in my heart? Do I cherish grudges; and have I refused to be reconciled? Are there uprisings within? Is it true that I still lose my temper? Does wrath hold me at times in its grip? Such a heart was foreign to Jesus Christ.

5. *Have I been delivered from jealousy and pride ?*

When another is preferred before me, does it make me envious and uncomfortable? Do I become jealous of those who can pray, speak and do things better than I can? Am I puffed up? Do I think a great deal of my own position and attainments? How free Jesus was from these things.

6. *Have I been delivered from lust and impurity of thought ?*

Do I allow my mind to harbour impure and unholy imaginations? Through the silent hours of the night, the lonely hours, am I addicted to such vices? Could we conceive of such a thing in the heart of Jesus?

It is not a question of Sinless Perfection, or Eradication. These phrases are neither in the Bible, nor have they been demonstrated in Christian experience. We believe in Christian Perfection; namely, that degree of holiness which is within the reach of man and which God expects His children to attain; but we do not believe in Godly, Angelic, or Sinless Perfection, for we still come short of the Divine standard—the glory of God.

Nor do we believe in Suppression. It is not a case of anger controlled. A story is told by Charles G. Turnbull of an old Quaker woman who had smiled most sweetly under a most distressing provocation. A young woman was with her at the time, and turning to the older one, exclaimed:

"I cannot understand how you were able to keep your temper."

"Ah!" exclaimed the Quaker woman, "thee didst not see the boiling inside."

And she thought that that was victory. She had been able to suppress her feelings and to control her anger so that no one could witness it. But whether on the inside or the outside, it really made no difference. It was a sin just the same, and so far as God was concerned, she might just as well have exploded; for He could see the boiling on the inside. The boiling was simply the outcome, the manifestation of sin. To control it did not make it less sinful. There is no victory in that. But, thank God, there is deliverance from all inward sins. God's children do not need to boil.

Dr. Simpson, so I am told, was one time listening to an argument between those who believed in Sinless Perfection and those who believed in Suppression. And as the debate waxed warmer and warmer, it was observed that something of a rather red hue was rising in the faces of both parties. The very thing that those who claimed Sinless Perfection or Eradication declared did not exist began to manifest itself in the heated words and rising colour of the speakers. And the others who taught Suppression seemed unconscious of the fact that somehow the cover had come off, and that it was not just then suppressed, at least not wholly so.

Finally, Dr. Simpson arose and spoke, "Brethren," he said, "it is not Eradication; and, brethren, it is not Suppression, but it is Habitation."

Thank God for Habitation! Oh, the joy of it! "Christ in you. Christ liveth in me. I in you." God-inhabited. "An habitation of God through the Spirit" (Eph. ii. 22). This is the secret—Christ our Victory. Hallelujah!

> In my heart the Saviour lives;
> Vict'ry over sin He gives;
> By His wondrous grace divine,
> Resurrection life is mine.
>
> Wondrous secret, yet how true,
> Christ the Saviour lives anew,
> Lives to reign within my heart
> And His risen life impart.
>
> Oh, how precious—can it be
> I in Him and He in me?
> Life abundant, life divine—
> God's eternal fullness mine.

In the old days it was victory, if any, with effort. Now it is victory without effort. Another has taken up the fight. "The battle is not yours but God's."

It is control now, not by self and will-power, but by Another. "When the enemy shall come in like a flood, the Spirit of the Lord will lift up a standard against him." Mark you, it is the Spirit who goes forth to meet the enemy now, and I hide behind the standard. Like the little girl who had just been saved. Jesus, she said, was in her heart. And when questioned as to what she would do if Satan knocked at the door, responded by saying: "Why, I would send Jesus to the door." She had the secret all right. "Ye shall not need to fight in this battle. Stand ye still and see the salvation of the Lord which He will work for you this day." Oh, glorious truth! The righteousness of the law is now fulfilled, not "by" us, but "in" us, by the Holy Spirit (Rom. viii. 4).

It is not our struggling to rid ourselves of the works of the flesh, not man's efforts to give up and get rid of sin; but being so filled with the Holy Spirit, so God-inhabited that we have no room for sin. In order to light a room, we do not drive the darkness out; but we let the light in, and, lo, the darkness disappears. Neither do we labour in the spring to remove all the dead leaves from the trees. That would be an impossible task. But by a law of nature there flows up the trunk the life-giving sap, and signs of new life soon appear. Then the old dead leaves just naturally fall off. At the bitter waters of Marah they did not cleanse the stream by trying to locate and get rid of whatever caused the bitterness; but they threw in the bough of a tree, and, lo, the waters became sweet. It is "the expulsive power of a new affection." The stronger destroys the weaker. The sweet expels the bitter. The light overpowers the darkness. "He that is in you is greater than he that is in the world." It is victory by Another. In Rom. vii it is "I," "ME," "MY" forty times, while in Rom. viii the Holy Spirit is mentioned nineteen times. He now indwells the believer and fights his battles.

"Art thou for us, or for our adversaries?" demanded Joshua of the man who stood over against Jericho.

"Nay," responded the One addressed, "but as Captain of the Lord's host am I now come."

"What saith my Lord to his servant?" cried Joshua, falling to the ground.

Why did he take such an attitude? Would we have acted so? Or would we have replied something like this:

"Well, Captain, I appreciate your offer; but really I do not need your help. I have a large army, well armed, and we are able to capture Jericho alone."

Had he said that Jericho never would have been taken. And yet this is what Christians are doing all the time. Self-effort, will-power, striving and struggling—these are our methods. But God tells us to lay down our weapons; stop trying, cease struggling, and let Him undertake. We are no match for the enemy. He alone can win the victory. "Christ in you"—this is our only hope. He defeated Satan at the Cross, and He can easily do it again.

Now shall we not "Let go and let God?" Admit our own inefficiency and weakness, and from this moment trust Him to undertake for us. He alone is sufficient. The drowning man who continues to struggle is hard to save. But the moment he has sense enough to give up, surrender, yield himself to the one who would rescue him, there is every hope. Self-effort can never avail. I live because

"Christ liveth in me." He is my victory. I trust Him. Praise the Lord.

The question is often asked: "Can victory be sustained?" Well, it is simply a matter of His keeping power. Is He able? Can He keep for a minute, for an hour? And if for one hour why not for a day? Then if Christ can keep His child victorious for a whole day, why not for a year? Ah, yes, thank God, there is uninterrupted victory!

It is a question of "looking unto Jesus." Peter looked at the waves, and immediately he began to sink. But as soon as he got his eyes on Jesus again he was safe. How often we look at the difficulties that surround us on every side! And seeing it is impossible for us to look two ways at once, we must of necessity take our eyes off Jesus in order to see our problems. Then to turn them on Him once more is to take them off the things around us. Keep "looking unto Jesus," and victory will be maintained.

As long as the trolley is on the wire, the car can keep going, but the moment the two are disconnected the car stops. We are not like storage batteries. God does not charge us up and set us going independent of Himself. We must keep in touch, in vital connection all the time, for we are "Kept by the power of God through faith" (1 Pet. i. 5). It is a faith life. "Without me, apart from me, severed from me, ye can do nothing," said Jesus.

As long as the Holy Spirit holds sway, just so long will victory be maintained. He can be slighted, grieved and quenched until He no longer dominates. "Ye shall receive power," declared Jesus, "when the Holy Ghost is come upon you." But then, "Walk in the Spirit, and ye shall not fulfil the lusts of the flesh." Power over sin? Yes. But sustained power by a sustained walk, yielded to and controlled by the Holy Spirit. "I will put my Spirit within you, and cause you to walk in my statutes."

The author of that beautiful hymn "Moment by Moment," said that the inspiration came to him from "I need Thee every hour." "That would never do," he declared, "I need Him every moment." And so he sat down and wrote those wonderful words that so perfectly set forth the secret of sustained victory:

> " Moment by moment I'm kept in His love.
> Moment by moment I've life from above.
> Looking to Jesus till glory doth shine,
> Moment by moment, O Lord, I am Thine."

This, then, is the life to which God is calling us, a life of victory over sin through the indwelling power of the Holy Spirit. Have we entered in? I have tried to be simple and clear in my presentation. It is now up to you to possess your possessions in Christ. You may continue in defeat, or you may live from this day a life of glorious victory. He can set you free and make you more than conqueror. You need not fail. "They do no iniquity," is the plain declaration of Scripture (Ps. cxix. 3). "These things write I unto you that ye SIN NOT" (1 John ii. 1). "Thy Word have I hid in mine heart, that I might not sin against Thee" (Ps. cxix. 2). If these verses mean anything, they mean that you and I do not need to commit conscious, known sin. And if we do, either in thought, word or deed, we are not living victorious lives. "But thanks be to God, which giveth us the *victory* through our Lord Jesus Christ" (1 Cor. xv. 57).

CHAPTER VI

WE are going to let God search us. We want to find out if possible just what He thinks of us. Our prayer will be the cry of the Psalmist, "Search me, O God, and know my heart; try me and know my thoughts; and see if there be any wicked way in me." And may He turn the searchlight of His Holy Spirit upon us until we are enabled to see ourselves as He sees us.

We are not trying to find out what the world thinks of us. Newspapers, books, and gossip may give the very opposite report of us to what God would give. They may praise while He condemns, or they may condemn where He praises. We are not even asking the opinion of our nearest and dearest friends. Even they may be deceived in us. "Man looketh on the outward appearance but God looketh on the heart." Our only desire is to discover what God thinks of us.

We shall some day stand face to face with God. And then, in the sight of the whole universe, we shall be unveiled and the innermost secrets of our hearts laid bare. The cloak that hid us from man will not hide us from God. Is it not better to find out now what He thinks of us, and if, as He weighs us in the balance we are found wanting, make up at once what we lack and get right with Him?

And so I ask, "What does God think of me?" God who searcheth the heart, as He looks into mine, what does He find there? Am I well pleasing in His sight? What does He think of me?

1. *What Does God Think of My Work?*

Does he find me genuine and sincere, free from all deception, and a stranger to hypocrisy? Never mind how much I blunder. The question is, Am I earnest? Am I sincere? If my motives are right, He will overlook my mistakes. Am I loyal to Him? Do I work from my heart, or are my labours merely professional? Is there any thought of personal gain? Am I selfish? Has money any influence in my decisions or plans? Would I serve Him just as earnestly if I got nothing out of it? Am I genuine?

Is my work counting for God? Does my life tell for Jesus? Am I able to lead others into a life of power and victory? Can I win souls to Christ? Do I ever try? Have I spoken to any one about his soul during the past year? Have I a message, or is my experience too shallow to mean anything to others? Do my unsaved friends know that I am a Christian?

2. *What Does God Think of My Social Relationships?*

Have I obeyed His summons, "Come out from among them, and be ye separate," and, "Be ye not unequally yoked together with unbelievers?" Are the things I am doing pleasing to Him? Can He smile upon me? Is there any pleasure that is driving Him from my heart and shutting out His presence? Is my conscience at rest, or does it trouble me when I do certain things and go to certain places? Am I willing to give up all for Jesus and to choose Him before the world? He gave up all for me. Do I want to please Him or am I going to argue the question with Him? Do I waste time that rightly belongs to Him? Are my evenings given up to social events when they are so much needed for His work?

3. *What Does God Think of My Devotional Life?*

Do I spend enough time with Him in private? Or am I hurried? Do I get alone with God? Do I love to meet Him in the inner chamber? Is communion with Him sweet to me? Is Jesus real? Does He fully satisfy?

Am I a student of God's Word? Do I study it in private, or is it all done in public? Does He unfold its secrets and make it real to me? Do I claim His promises and make them mine?

Is my life saturated with Prayer? Do I pray and get answers? Have I learned how to pray? Do I merely say prayers, or do I pray? And are my prayers availing? Is prayer a real, vital thing to me?

4. *What Does God Think of My Christian Progress?*

Am I making progress in Spiritual things? Am I a growing Christian? Am I better this year than last? Is Jesus more real to me? Can my friends see any difference in me? Are the old weaknesses and failings of the flesh disappearing, and is the fruit of the Spirit becoming increasingly mine?

Am I making progress against sin, especially my besetting sin? Has it been conquered, the sin that at one time conquered me? Do I want to be delivered from it? Is there still some cherished idol shutting out His peace and power, His presence, sunshine and love? Do I believe that He is able to keep me from falling, that all power is His?

And now, having honestly faced these four vital questions, what is the answer? We often testify that Jesus satisfies. But suppose we turn it around and ask, "Is *He* satisfied? Is God pleased with me?" For all that matters, all that is important, is our Lord's estimate of us. Has He been disappointed, or are we pleasing in His sight? Does He take delight in us? *What does God think of me?*

CHAPTER VII

THE SURRENDERED LIFE

WHEN I talk about Surrender I like to be definite. It sometimes pays to go into detail. And so I am going to be very plain and simple in order that you may have no hazy idea as to what I mean, for the Surrendered Life involves the laying of everything on God's altar.

1. *Self*.

What would a man think of a young woman who in response to his appeal, offered her lover lands and houses or anything else she owned? Would he be satisfied? Not for a moment. He is not asking for her possessions; he is asking for herself. Nor will any substitute satisfy. And so it is with Jesus Christ. He wants us, body and soul, spirit. Hence, we must first of all lay ourselves on the altar, and say, "I'll go where you want me to go, dear Lord. To India, Africa or China. To be a missionary or a minister. I'll forsake all and answer Thy Call."

> " Take myself and I will be
>   Ever, only, all for Thee."

2. *Loved Ones.*

Having placed myself on God's altar, I now bring my loved ones, my son or daughter, my father or mother. If the Lord wants my child for the foreign field He may have her. If He demands that I leave father and mother, I obey. Even if He should choose to take my loved one to Himself I dare not murmur, "Thy will be done."

"Why am I not happy?" inquired a wealthy lady as she stood beside the great missionary, Dr. Jonathan Goforth, of China, in her home.

"Have you surrended all?" inquired the man of God, quietly.

"Yes, so far as I know, I have surrendered all," responded the woman.

"Are you sure," insisted Dr. Goforth, "that your all is on the altar?"

"My all is on the altar, I believe," answered the woman again.

"And you would be willing for God to take your little girl here and send her to China?" asked the missionary, placing his hand on her head.

"God take my daughter and make her a missionary in China! I should say not. I want her here with me," exclaimed the mother.

"And yet you tell me you have surrendered all, and you haven't even given your own child to God. How can you expect God's peace and blessing? You stand as it were between God and His will for your daughter, and you say to Him, 'Thus far shalt Thou come and no farther. You can have my home; You can have my money; You can have me, but— don't touch my daughter.' Madam, do you call that surrender?"

3. *Talents.*

Our talents were never given to be used for ourselves. God's gifts are to be invested for Him. What right have we to use them selfishly? Once we catch God's vision, never again will we use our talents along worldly lines. You may have a talent for elocution, oratory, speaking. The question is: How are you using it? Is it simply for the purpose of amusing and entertaining? Or has it been invested for God? You may be gifted in writing. But what and for whom are you writing? Is it for the world, or for God? Are you writing for money or for the Kingdom? It may be you have been given the talent of making money. But remember, "It is God that giveth thee power to get wealth." Then for whom are you making money? For yourself or for God? Or your talent may be that of song. God has given you a voice. Are you using it in concerts to please your friends? Do you sing the songs of the world? Or, can Jesus Christ proclaim His message to burdened, sin-sick souls, through your talent of song? Frances Ridley Havergal sang:

> " Take my voice and let me sing
>   Always, only, for my King."

4. *Time.*

"Redeeming the time." What a responsibility! What are we doing with our time, our spare hours? Do we invest it for God or use it for selfish pursuits that don't count? Somehow we seem to have time for everything else in the world, time to eat and

time to sleep, time to shop and time to talk, time for
the newspaper and time for our visitors, time for
pleasure and time for work, but no time for God.
Do we spend our time entertaining our friends,
providing expensive dinner parties, and whiling away
the hours in idle talk? Or, do we live as pilgrims
and act like sojourners? Are we different from the
world? Are the precious hours given to conversation
about Himself, and the interest of the Kingdom?
Thus will it be when the Holy Spirit comes. Let us
stop, and begin right now to practise what we sing:

> " All for Jesus! all for Jesus!
> All my days and all my hours."

5. *Money.*

Not a tenth, but all. Everything we own belongs
to God and we are only stewards. Then it behoves
us to watch how we spend it. Does it go for luxury
or for missions; for non-necessities or for the evangelization of the world? Do we spend it on ourselves
to gratify our selfish desires, or is it held and used
in God's work? Are we simply banking it to leave
to someone who is quite able to take care of himself? Or are we investing it as God's steward in the
souls of men? Do we build homes far larger than
we need? Are we paying $100 per month rent,
when we could manage equally as well in a house
that would only cost $60? No wonder we have
nothing for God! Oh, but the reckoning day is near.
The accounting time will come. I would not like
to meet Him with a large bank account. That
would be a terrible calamity. He expects me to

invest it somehow before I die, for Him. Not, "How much of my money will I give to God," but, "How much of God's money will I keep for myself?" Some day he will call us to account for our steward-ship. Our money, then, must also be placed on God's altar.

> " Take my silver and my gold,
>   Not a mite would I withhold."

Well, now, will you lay your all on the altar? Are you ready to yield, to dedicate, to consecrate every-thing? Oh, that you would take this initial step! Be definite. Make a whole-hearted surrender of your life to God. Hold nothing back. Yield up your will and accept His. Have no plans of your own. Go where He wants you to go and be what He wants you to be. All your cherished hopes, all your personal ambitions—give Him yourself. There can be no substitute for your act of surrender. You must pay the price. No compromise is possible. Abandon your life to God. He requires an empty vessel. How can He fill it if it is already full? Can a room be full of pure air and foul at the same time?

A BLANK AGREEMENT

It is a question of signing a blank agreement. Put your name down at the bottom and let God write in the terms and conditions of the agreement after. He will only put down one step at a time and when you take that the next will be made plain. Trust Him, then, to plan your life and to fill in the agreement after you have signed it.

c

SEALED ORDERS

It means that you sail under sealed orders. Where, you do not know. When, you cannot say. Why, is not your business. How, must not concern you. It is yours to accept from Him the sealed orders containing His great blue print for your life, and to open and read them just when and just as much at a time as He wills.

AN ETERNAL "YES"

It is saying an eternal "Yes" to God. An eternal "No" to self and "Yes" to Him. And it must be so final that it holds good all the rest of your life. "Lord, what wilt Thou have me to do? Where wilt Thou have me to go?" He dictates and you obey. One great, final, eternal, glorious Yes, and the question is forever settled. Then just keep saying "Yes" all along the way.

> " Lord, I give myself to Thee,
> Friends and time and earthly store;
> Soul and body Thine to be—
> Wholly Thine for evermore."

CHAPTER VIII

THE SANCTIFIED LIFE

IT is not my purpose to go into the doctrinal side of Sanctification, for I have learned that it is possible to know an experience doctrinally and yet fail to appropriate it in a practical way. Therefore I am going to be very simple and emphasize the experimental side of a sanctified life.

And first of all, I want to tell you three things that Sanctification is not, in order that you may the easier comprehend what it is.

First, it is not freedom from temptation. The probability is that you will be tempted more as you live the sanctified life than ever before. Until then you have not been very dangerous to the kingdom of Satan; consequently he has not bothered much with you. But the moment you enter this experience he will do everything in his power to defeat you. Hence, Sanctification by no means ensures freedom from temptation. Let him that is spiritual consider himself lest he also be tempted.

Second, it is not a guarantee of safety from the possibility of sin. "Let him that thinketh he standeth take heed lest he fall." There is no condition in this life where a Christian is safe from the possibility of sin. Those who rise highest can fall lowest. Beware, then, of a false security, for Sanctification does not guarantee safety from the possibility of sin.

Third, it is not a gradual deliverance from sin. That is never God's way of victory. Sin is dealt with, settled with, done with once for all. If a drunkard had been in the habit of taking five glasses of liquor a day, you would not dream of advising him to take four to-morrow, three the next day, two the next, then one, etc. You know that there must be a crisis moment when he deliberately turns from it and stops. And so with Sanctification, sin's power is broken and you yield no more.

Now having told you what it is not, let me mention three things that it is:

First, it is an instantaneous crisis experience. That means it has a beginning, and while you may view it as a process life-long in its result, you must also recognize its crisis nature. There must be a beginning; it must have a start. The children of Israel found the crossing of the Jordan just such an experience. It was a crisis hour in their history. In the morning they were on the wilderness side; in the evening they were on the opposite bank.

Second, it is a life of victory over sin. If it is not that, it is nothing. God has guaranteed deliverance from the power of sin. "Sin shall not have dominion over you." Apart from a life of victory over sin a profession of sanctification is a mockery.

Third, it is a life-long transformation into Christlikeness. "We all, with open face beholding as in a glass the glory of the Lord, are changed into the same image from glory to glory, even as by the Spirit of the Lord" (2 Cor. iii. 18). More and more we partake of His image until at last when He shall appear we shall be like Him.

When does Sanctification take place? In God's plan at conversion, but in man's experience, as a rule, after. I do not believe that God intends His children to wander for years in the wilderness. It is His purpose that they should yield so fully at conversion and live such a Spirit-filled life ever after that back-sliding would be unknown. Unfortunately very few do, and the result is that there must come a second great crisis when they turn from failure and disappointment in absolute surrender to live only and wholly for God.

What does Sanctification mean? The word itself simply means "to set apart"; and anything "set apart" from a common to a sacred use, whether animate or inanimate, is sanctified. Your life belongs to God. What He wants you to do is to recognize this fact, acquiesce in it, and set yourself apart for the high and holy purpose intended.

There are three steps in Sanctification, and there are two parts to the experience. I am speaking now, not of the doctrinal but rather of the practical side. From a theological standpoint you may not understand it, and yet you may know it experimentally. And that is the only thing that matters after all.

Now from a practical standpoint there are, as I have already stated, two sides to the experience known as Sanctification. There is first man's part and second, God's part.

A very significant statement is found in Joshua iii. 5, where the command is given, "Sanctify yourselves." "But," you exclaim, "I always thought that Sanctification was a work of the Holy Spirit." Then how do you explain this very clear and definite injunction, "Sanctify yourselves"? The problem is not hard to solve. This is man's part. And before God can possibly do His part, man must do his, and sanctify himself.

I have also stated that there are three steps in Sanctification. The first two constitute man's side of the transaction, and the third, God's. These three steps, very simply worded, are: (1) Separation; (2) Dedication; (3) Filling. First "separation from," second, "dedication to," third, "filling with."

You see, it means not only a "separation from," but also a "dedication to." Separation is the negative side, dedication the positive. There are two parts to man's side of sanctification. "Sanctify yourselves." You do your part and God will do His. The third step is "filling with." But this is God's part. And the reason so many pray and plead and wait in vain for the "filling with" is simply because they have not yet taken both the steps demanded by God upon which the third depends.

Let us then first of all be sure that our separation is complete. God insists upon a clean cut separation from sin in every shape and form, from the world and all its allurements, from everything that grieves the Holy Spirit and cripples our power. Nor can we fool Him. He knows whether or not we mean what we say. Is then our separation complete? And if not let us begin at once to go all the way.

Second, we must dedicate our lives to God. Separation is incomplete unless it involves this second step. We separate from the old self life and all that is displeasing to God only that we may be separated unto Him. Hence, dedication means the setting of one's self apart for God. We are to be holy; that is, we are separated unto God for a holy purpose. This dedication must be made actual and real in our experience.

Is, then, our all on the altar? Have we dedicated ourselves and all we possess, to God? Or, are we holding something back? It may be our money, our talents, some loved one; but whatever it is there will be no "filling with" until it has been fully and eternally dedicated to God. Only then can God do His part and fill with the Holy Spirit. When our all is on the altar the fire of God will fall.

Now, when you know positively, when you are absolutely sure that you have taken these first two steps after waiting before God long enough for the Holy Spirit to search you, then by simple faith without any outward manifestation whatever, you can believe the Word, and rise from your knees knowing that God has done His part.

Listen: "What things soever ye desire, when ye pray, *believe* that ye *receive* them, and ye shall have them" (Mark xi. 24). He doesn't tell you to believe you are *going* to receive them, but to believe that ye *receive*, right there and then, that moment, the instant you believe.

Now don't let Satan cheat you out of the blessing by making you wait for some supernatural manifestation or feeling. You will know the joy and comfort of the Holy Spirit as you go out believing, testifying, acting on your faith. God's order for Sanctification is the same as for Salvation. First, "fact"; second, "faith"; third, "feeling." Now Satan always reverses the Divine order, and tells you to look for feeling. But how can you feel before you believe and how can you believe until you know something to believe?

Here are some facts: "If we confess our sins, He is faithful and just to forgive us our sins, and to cleanse us from all unrighteousness" (1 Jn. i. 9).

The condition is that you confess. Have you met the condition? Then, why make God a liar? "If we walk in the light, as He is in the light, we have fellowship one with another, and the blood of Jesus Christ His Son cleanseth us from all sin" (1 Jn. i. 7). What is the condition? "If we walk in the light." And what happens? "The blood of Jesus Christ, His Son, cleanseth us from all sin." "But," you say, "I don't feel cleansed." No, and you never will until you first of all believe God's Word and act on your faith. Here is the third great fact:—"How much more shall your heavenly Father give the Holy Spirit to them that ask Him?" (Luke xi. 13). The condition? "Ask." Have you conscientiously taken the first two steps? Then ask. And feel? No, believe. God is on the giving hand. He delights to bless. "How much more!"

"Lord Jesus, I separate from all that is displeasing in Thy sight, and I dedicate myself and all I possess to Thee. And now, Lord, I believe Thy Word. Thou hast said, 'Whatsoever things ye desire when ye pray believe that ye receive them, and ye shall have them.' Lord, I desire from this moment to live a sanctified life, free from the power of sin, filled with the Holy Spirit, and one hundred per cent. for Thee.

' I want, dear Lord, a heart that's true and clean,
A sunlit heart, with not a cloud between:
A heart like Thine, a heart divine, a heart as white
    as snow—
On me, dear Lord, a heart like this bestow.'

"And so, Lord Jesus, without any feeling, without any evidence or special manifestation, having taken the first two steps and thus met the conditions, I do here and now believe that I am forgiven, the blood does cleanse me, even me, from all sin, the Holy Spirit comes, and I do receive Him into my heart and life to fill me to the uttermost. Thou dost accept me; Thou, O Christ, art now my Sanctification, and I am complete in Thee. Blessed be Thy name!

' Lord, I believe. Lord, I believe,
  Saviour raise my faith in Thee till it can move a mountain;
  Lord, I believe; Lord, I believe,
  All my doubts are buried in the fountain.' "

Yes, praise God! I have seen scores enter into this experience by taking these simple steps. It works, and that is the best of it. Here is a man who has a violent temper. For less than ten minutes he kneels at the altar, and takes the steps that I have mentioned one by one. Then without emotion of any kind he testifies to what God has done. Does it work and will it last? Oh, hallelujah! Week after week he gives a glowing testimony, declaring that his temper is gone, and that he is living in Sanctification day by day. His whole life has been revolutionized, utterly changed.

May God enable you to take these simple steps and thus enter into the glorious experience of the Sanctified Life.

CHAPTER IX

THE LORDSHIP OF JESUS

THERE are many to whom Jesus Christ is Saviour but not Lord; many who have been saved by Jesus who have never recognised Him as Master. But not until He has been given that place will He be satisfied.

In Luke xiv. 25, He lays down the terms of discipleship. But first of all let me say that to be a disciple in the true sense of the word means much more than forgiveness. A disciple is a learner, one who follows after and who recognizes another as master.

In the second place let me say that the Lord Jesus Christ has the absolute right to lay down the terms upon which He will accept followers as His disciples. In the days of the Great War when conscription was in vogue, men were compelled to serve whether they wanted to or not, but before the days of conscription every man had the privilege of deciding for himself. Now the government had the right to lay down the terms upon which men would be enlisted as soldiers, but the man himself after reading the terms had the power to accept or reject as he saw fit. That did not mean that he was no longer a citizen of his country. It simply meant that he refused to serve.

And, so with you, my friend. You may belong to Jesus Christ and be a citizen of heaven and still refuse to acknowledge Him as your Lord and Master and place yourself under His orders in glad obedience. You may be saved and yet not be a disciple.

Now let us look at the passage in Luke xiv. 25–27. It reads as follows: "And there went great multitudes with Him: and He turned, and said unto them." I wonder what you would have done! What would you have said? If I know anything about human nature you would have spoken words to please your followers. But Jesus Christ never hid the cross. If the road was thorny He always said so.

"If any man come to Me, and hate not his father, and mother, and wife, and children, and brethren, and sisters, yea, and his own life also, he cannot be my disciple. And whosoever does not bear his cross, and come after Me, cannot be my disciple." "But," you exclaim, "does Jesus Christ mean that a man must hate his loved ones in order to be His disciple?" Let us turn to Matt. x. 37. Here we have the same term of discipleship but in somewhat different language. It reads thus: "He that loveth father and mother *more* than Me is not worthy of Me: and he that loveth son or daughter *more* than Me is not worthy of Me."

What, then are the terms of discipleship? Let me give the answer in just two words: "GOD FIRST." And if I could, I would put them on a banner in the sight of every congregation in the world—GOD FIRST.

Now let us ask ourselves some very plain questions. Does God come first in my life or does business hold the supreme place? Is it God first or pleasure? God first or money? What about my family, my loved ones? Do they come first or does God? All difficulties can thus be solved and all problems settled. No

longer do I need to ask: Is it right to go here or there?
May I take part in this pleasure or that? One
decision only: God First!

I remember a mother who would not put God first,
and to-day the body of her daughter lies in the
cemetery. She had asked her mother if she might
answer God's call and go to the foreign field. The
mother agreed on condition that she would continue
to work for three or four months. Then at the end of
that time she went back on her word, broke her
promise and refused to let her daughter go. Less than
a year passed before God, whom she would not recognize as Lord, came and took her daughter to Himself.

Now the man who puts God first in his life and
takes up the cross to faithfully follow his Lord and
Master will have fulfilled the first conditions of
discipleship.

> " Where he leads me I will follow,
>   I'll go with Him all the way."

The last condition of discipleship is found in Luke
xiv. 33. It reads as follows: " Whosoever he be of you
that forsaketh not all that he hath, he cannot be My
disciple." "But," you exclaim, "that condition is
almost impossible to meet. Do you mean to say that
God asks His followers to literally forsake everything? If so, then I am not His disciple, for I still
have a home, a wife and a small bank account.
Am I to forsake these?"

In the Revised Version you will find that the word
"forsake" has been translated "renounce." Now let
us read it: "Whosoever he be of you that *renounceth*
not all that he hath, he cannot be My disciple." It is
one thing to renounce; it is another to forsake. God

demands that His children renounce everything whereas He may ask them to actually forsake very few of the things they have renounced.

To renounce a thing means to relinquish all claim. The best example is probably found in Acts iv. 32: "Neither said any of them that aught of the things that he possessed was his own."

Nothing that I am or own belongs to me. All is God's. He allows me the use of it as it pleases Him, but He has the first, the supreme claim. Recognizing that, I gladly place all at His disposal, take my hands off, and own Him as Lord. Having definitely relinquished all claim, I deliberately turn my back on everything. Thus I renounce all that I am and have. It is no longer mine but God's. Henceforth He has the absolute right to do what He likes with it, and if at any time He should call upon me to literally forsake what I have renounced I must not even murmur or complain. I give Him all my children. He may take one or none to the foreign field and thus demand that I forsake those whom I have already renounced. So with my money and everything else.

No sooner will I renounce all than God will test me to see if my renunciation is genuine. It was so with Abraham. He had renounced Isaac, recognizing that he belonged to God alone. Then God demanded the sacrifice on Mount Moriah and Abraham never flinched. His renunciation was thereby proven to be genuine. It will not be hard when the test comes if the renunciation has been real. But if it has only been a fake the testing time will be terrible, and in all probability the thing that was supposed to have been renounced will be taken back. Discipleship demands renunciation.

Remember, Jesus must be Lord of all, or not Lord at all. No man ever works for two firms at the same time. No slave owns two masters at once. Beware lest when you give Him a secondary place as you think, you awaken some day when it is too late to discover that He is not there at all. For He must be Lord of all, or not Lord at all. "No man can serve two masters."

"Suffer me first," said the young man to Jesus. Oh no, not "me first"—God First! My interests must always come second to His; never first. "Seek ye first the Kingdom of God."

Dr. Graham Scroggie, of Edinburgh, was one time speaking along this line, and at the close of the service he was approached by a young woman, a professing Christian, who had been greatly stirred.

"And why don't you yield?" inquired Dr. Scroggie.

"I am afraid I would have to do two things if I did," responded the girl.

"What are they?" questioned the minister.

"I play the piano in a concert hall, and I fear I would have to give it up," explained the inquirer.

"And the other?"

"I am afraid God would send me to China as a missionary."

Dr. Scroggie was wise in his dealings with the anxious. Opening his Bible at Acts x. 14, he explained to the young woman the absurdity of Peter's answer. A slave never dictates. And to say, "Not so," and then add the word "Lord," was impossible.

"Now," said Dr. Scroggie, "I want you to cross out the two words, 'Not so,' and leave the word 'Lord'; or else cross out 'Lord' and leave 'not so'."

Handing her his pencil he quietly walked away.

For two hours she struggled. Then he returned. Looking over her shoulder he saw a tear-stained page, but the words "Not so" were crossed out. With a glad light in her eyes she left the church and went home repeating over and over the one word, "Lord." No longer would she dictate. She was now His disciple and He her Lord and Master. Henceforth it would be, "Even so, Father," and, "Lord, what wilt Thou have me to do?"

"Lovest thou Me more than these?" And I can imagine Jesus pointing to the boats and nets, then to the other disciples, and finally to Peter's home and loved ones. "Peter, who comes first? Do I? Lovest thou Me more than these?" And that is the question He is asking still. Shall we, then, yield all, and crown Him Lord?

> " All hail the power of Jesus' Name!
>   Let Angels prostrate fall;
>   Bring forth the royal diadem
>   And crown Him Lord of all."

CHAPTER X

JUST IN TIME

"COULD you come to see a sick woman?"

"Is it urgent?"

"Yes, very; she may not live through the night."

"All right, I'll come at once," and I hung up the receiver.

Making my way through the city streets, I was soon at the place, and was taken immediately to the sick chamber. A woman with a sad and forlorn expression on her face looked up at me as I entered. She tried to speak, but her voice was so weak and broken that I had to bend low to catch the words she uttered. And I felt that I was already standing in the presence of the Angel of Death, for it was plain to see that her life was fast ebbing away. Hopelessness was depicted on her countenance while she waited for me to speak; and the darkness seemed to deepen as I watched the pale, drawn face, enshrouded in the gloom of almost hopeless despair. There was no time to lose—no time to talk of the things of this world: her eternal destiny was at stake.

"Mrs. C——, are you ready to go; have you any hope?" I enquired, as I bent over her.

"No, none," she murmured, shaking her head, while a deep-drawn sigh escaped her lips.

I stated as plainly as I could the wonderful plan

of salvation, and, kneeling down, prayed with her,
and then sang in tones subdued and low:

> " Just as I am—without one plea,
> But that thy blood was shed for me,
> And that Thou bidd'st me come to Thee,
>   O Lamb of God, I come!

> " Just as I am—and waiting not
> To rid my soul of one dark blot,
> To Thee, whose blood can cleanse each spot,
>   O Lamb of God, I come!"

As I sang the second verse, I heard her feeble
voice—broken, weak and wavering—trying to sing
with me. Sometimes I could distinguish the words,
but more often they were unintelligible, until I
came to the last line, and then she sang with heart
and voice:
>   " O Lamb of God, I come!"

And she did come—came in full assurance of faith;
and I left her, knowing that all was well, and that
she was going home to God.

And yet she was a member of the church, a member
but—unconverted. Conversion was her one great
need, for the Word of God plainly and emphatically
states that, "Except ye be converted, ye shall not
enter into the kingdom of heaven" (Matt. xviii. 3).
And as I went home, my heart was sad within me,
and I groaned aloud as I thought of the awful
responsibility resting upon ministers who allow
people to become members of churches without
being "born again."

I never saw Mrs. C—— again until I stood by
her casket and looked down upon her face, cold in
death. And as I preached her funeral sermon, I

determined more than ever to lay aside everything else and give myself unreservedly to the one great work of getting people ready for Heaven. The Word of God declares that "Christ Jesus came into the world to save sinners" (1 Tim. i. 15). This was His supreme purpose, not to reform them, not to improve them,—but to save them. Is there, then, anything else so urgent, so vitally important, as the salvation of an immortal soul? Did not the Saviour Himself declare that, "Except ye be converted, ye shall not enter into the kingdom of heaven?" Then let us believe God's Word, and be warned thereby.

.   .   .   .   .

Two or three days passed and again the telephone rang. This time it was a young man. He, too, was very sick, and had passed through intense suffering.

"Why have you sent for me?" I inquired.

"Because I am not ready to go; I am unsaved, and I want to get right with God," was his reply, or words to that effect.

Once again I told the old, old Story, and oh, how eagerly he drank it in! Text after text was quoted and explained, until at last he, also, saw and believed. Then I knelt in prayer, and closed by singing once more that matchless hymn:

> "Just as I am—Thou wilt receive,
>   Wilt welcome, pardon, cleanse, relieve.
>   Because Thy promise I believe,
>   O Lamb of God, I come!
>
> " Just as I am—Thy love unknown
>   Has broken every barrier down—
>   Now to be Thine, yea, Thine alone,
>   O Lamb of God, I come!"

He, too, sang the faith-inspiring words—words that made the way so plain; and he, too, came to Jesus, came as a lost and guilty sinner, and gave himself to the sinner's Saviour. Then I left him—left him fully satisfied and perfectly contented, his soul flooded with the love of God.

Next time I called he was unconscious; and the next—I buried him. Only one opportunity, only one chance. And what if I had talked of other things and left him lying there still unsaved, expecting to visit him again? And once more I resolved to spend my life in labouring for the souls of men, and to proclaim on every side with even greater earnestness, the awful, solemn warning that "Except ye be converted, ye shall not enter into the kingdom of heaven."

.   .   .   .   .

It was morning; seven o'clock. The phone rang loud and long. I answered, and the word from the other end almost took my breath.

"Miss H—— passed away at six o'clock this morning."

"Miss H——, what? dead!" I was stunned.

Two days ago she had phoned my wife and seemed in the best of spirits. The day before she was at her work in one of the departments of the T. Eaton Co., Toronto, and went home at the usual hour. On the way she stopped at the home of a friend, and after chatting pleasantly for some time, she sat down at the piano and sang with deep feeling the words of that beautiful hymn, "Open My Eyes, that I May See." Little did she realise how soon the prayer would be answered! Upon reaching home she ate a hearty supper, and about eight o'clock complained of being tired, and went to bed. At ten the doctor was called, and at three the minister and her relatives; at six she was gone. The night before she had walked into the house apparently strong and well; twenty-four hours later she was carried out in her casket, never to return.

Dead! and only three hours' warning, and I had never spoken to her about her soul. And yet some say I am too serious, that I should give myself more to social service, and the physical needs of the people; that I am always harping on soul-saving!

Great God, have mercy! and give us a glimpse of a soul lost, for is it not a fact that in spite of these awful warnings that occur almost daily, we still seem to forget that the Holy Spirit has written in God's unchangeable Word that "Except ye be converted, ye shall not enter into the kingdom of heaven?" And, "Except a man be born again, he cannot see the kingdom of God" (John iii. 3).

Let us believe the Bible, and we will no longer be indifferent; in the face of such solemn truths we must be serious. People are serious enough when a house is on fire; they do not think of taking time to wash and dress the children before they carry them to safety. Their one cry is "Save, save, or they perish!" And when we truly believe God's Word, believe that "Except ye be converted, ye shall not enter into the kingdom of heaven"; that souls are perishing all around, and that they will be lost eternally—when we really believe in our hearts, we will care about little else but getting them saved, and that as quickly as possible.

CHAPTER XI

THERE are two great essentials in the propagation of the Gospel—the messenger, and the message. The more I observe Christian activity and watch results, the more I am convinced that the most potent factor in it all has to do with personality. Character is the pivot upon which the wheels of Christianity turn. The messenger himself is, first and last, the key to the situation. There are men who will succeed in almost any parish. There are others who will fail no matter where they go. Unless the messenger be a man of God he must of necessity discover sooner or later that his efforts are in vain.

But we are not concerned just now with the man, important as he is. The words to which I want to draw your attention have to do, not with the messenger, but with his message. "Then Philip went down to the city of Samaria and *preached Christ* unto them" (Acts viii. 5). Now,

WHAT IS MEANT BY "PREACHING CHRIST?"

Perhaps if I answer first of all in a negative way we shall better understand the full significance of the phrase. First, then, let me say that "preaching Christ" does not mean merely preaching *about* Christ. A man may know all about the historic Jesus and yet not know Christ. He may be familiar with the incidents of His life from the cradle to the grave; he may even go further than that—he may believe and accept as genuine every event recorded in the Scriptures about Christ; he may believe everything that Jesus taught; the life of the Saviour may be as familiar to him as his own and yet he may not know Christ.

Men are resting upon an intellectual belief in the doctrines, creeds, dogmas, ceremonies, and sacraments of the Church, instead of in the person of Christ Himself. Doctrine is all right in its place; we could not exist without it. Creeds and dogmas were necessary in the early centuries of Christianity. Even the regular ceremonies of church worship are oftentimes helpful; and yet, the man who builds on this as a foundation for Eternity, will some day awake to the fact that he has built on shifting sand. They can never take the place of the living Christ.

I know of men who only attend church on communion Sunday. Now if Christianity has never brought to their conscience a sense of service, a love for prayer; if their attendance twelve times a year is to be taken as a test of their spirituality, then there is something radically wrong. If they come to church merely as a matter of form, I am afraid they have never, never experienced the grace of God. When Jesus Christ saves a man He always puts a desire for service in his heart. And so instead of attending only on communion Sunday, he will be there often, not because it is his duty, but because he loves God's house, and loves to serve.

Have you forgotten that almost the entire civilized world holds an intellectual belief in Christ? Do you realize that even the very devils believe and tremble? And if men, my friends, are going to rest on creeds and doctrines, forms and ceremonies, or even the ordinances of the church, or upon any knowledge they may possess *about* Christ, let me say most emphatically that they have never known Christ. For all these things, good though they may be, do not take the place of Christ. And so the preaching of them does not constitute "preaching Christ."

But further,—"preaching Christ" does not mean the reading of religious essays, the delivering of popular lectures, reviewing new books, discussing present-day politics, socialism, or economics. They are all needful. I do not for a moment condemn any of them, but I do condemn the bringing of them into the pulpit. Some of our pulpits to-day are given over to Sunday Evening Clubs, our churches are becoming lecture halls, and evangelism, the work of saving men, is considered out of date. For when God desires to send a mighty revival to our city, the doors of our churches (not all, thank God!) are closed, and our minds steeled against it. Is it any wonder that so many of our churches are empty, our pulpits powerless, and our efforts inefficient?

My brethren! "preaching Christ" means proclaiming Him as a crucified, resurrected, ascended, and living Saviour. You notice that I emphasize each word,—*crucified*, *resurrected*, *ascended*, and *living* Saviour. I do not leave out His earthly life, His works, teachings and character. I merely emphasize the most important facts of all—His death and resurrection. Thank God, He is living

at this present moment, possessing all power and
authority, and ready to enter into vital relationship
with every life. A present Saviour. I want you to
think of Jesus as living to-day. I do not bring
you a dead and powerless Christ, but a present,
living Saviour. A Saviour who at this moment can
enter into the most hopeless heart of the most hopeless man in all the world, and so change and trans-
form him, that he will ever afterwards live a new
life. Jesus is here to-day, and He is here to save. Do
you see what I mean? Have I in any sense made
Christ real to you? If only I could make you realise
that you must deal with a living person, and not with
a dead Christ! My friends, it is when I present
Christ to you in this way that I am "preaching
Christ."

WHY PREACH CHRIST?

But why are we to preach Christ? There are two
reasons, both of paramount importance. First,
because it is our business. The business of a farmer
is to be a farmer, not a banker. The business of a
lawyer is to be a lawyer, not a doctor. If you
had the misfortune to have a lawsuit you would
probably engage a lawyer. But what would you
do if the plumbing broke? Go to the lawyer again?
certainly not. You would immediately send for a
plumber. And why? Simply because it is a plumber's
business to be a plumber. And it is the business
of the Christian to *preach Christ*.

Every Mohammedan trader is a missionary. You
may find him pressing down into the Sudan of
Central Africa, or out on the sands of the Arabian
desert. It matters not. He buys and sells as he

goes along, but he never neglects an opportunity of propagating his faith. And why? Simply because he is a Mohammedan and it is his business to spread Mohammedanism.

Let us go back for a moment to the passage in the eighth chapter of Acts. The record is that "they went everywhere preaching the Word." They! Who? The twelve apostles? No. As a matter of fact the twelve did not go at all. They remained at headquarters. "They" means the entire body of Christian believers, thousands in number. And these ordinary laymen and laywomen were scattered abroad, and went everywhere, doing what? Hiding, keeping quiet? No. They went everywhere *preaching*. Don't you see? It was their business. God nowhere declares that only the ministers are to preach the Glad Tidings. His command is to all.

And "preaching" does not mean that they delivered a formal discourse from the pulpit. The use of that word has greatly changed. It simply means "telling the Story." Telling it man to man, individual to individual. Telling it anyway, and anywhere, but telling it. Philip journeys to Gaza, and meets an Ethiopian eunuch. Soon he has told him the story of Jesus, and the eunuch is baptized. His audience was composed of only one man. And yet the Word plainly states that "he began at the same Scripture and *preached* unto him Jesus." That is what is meant by "preaching." Can we not do it? My friends, it is our *business to preach Christ*.

But there is still another reason, and it is this,— preach Christ because He is the only Remedy for sin. Men have striven for centuries in every conceivable way to rid themselves of sin, and have failed. Failed because they did not know the One,

and the ONLY One who was able to free them.
Mohammed cannot save. Confucius cannot save.
Buddha cannot save. Jesus Christ CAN. Yea,
more, He will! That was what He came for. That
was why He died. And to Him and Him alone, I
bid you come, for "there is none other name under
heaven given among men, whereby we must be
saved" (Acts iv. 12). And if that be true, then it
behoves us one and all, clergy and laity alike, to
PREACH CHRIST.

CHAPTER XII

WHICH IS YOUR GOAL?

"HOW do you find the work among the Indians now?" I enquired of a missionary on the Pacific Coast.

"Oh, harder, much harder," was the reply. "Many of them have begun to doubt the Bible and to question the Christian religion. They have lost faith."

"Why! how is that?" I asked, wondering what his explanation would be.

"The war—Christian nations fighting each other —the Indians can't understand it." And his face grew solemn as he looked out over the mountain ranges across the channel.

And my heart, too, was saddened for I knew what he did not, knew that it was due not at all to the war, but to the unscriptural teaching of the present day that not only the Indians but the heathen of every foreign land as well as thousands in our so-called Christian countries have lost faith and are perplexed.

It is only occasionally that I preach on the pre-millennial Coming of Christ, because I recognize that it is a truth and not the great central truth of Christianity. It is not the Gospel. I am forced to admit that it is the pivot point upon which a man's ministry is bound to turn. I find that the goal for which he works makes all the difference in the world as to the methods he uses and the results he hopes to obtain.

For instance, if his goal is the Conversion of the World, and if he believes this to be the work of the Church, then he is going to labour on until that goal is reached. He will expect to see conditions improving and Christianity advancing on every side. And if such is not the case, he is bound to be cast down, pessimistic, discouraged and disappointed.

Were I a post millennialist to-day, in view of the tragic struggle that has recently terminated, I would be the most pessimistic, discouraged and disappointed person in the world. To think of the awful set-back that Christianity has received, to meet the thousands whom I have met this summer who have lost faith, and who speak contemptuously of our Christian (?) nations and the Christian religion, instead of a glorious conquest and the spread of righteousness, would be enough to make me lose all hope of the ultimate christianization of the human race. If I believed that the Conversion of the World was the task of the Church, and the goal for which I must strive, I would give up in despair.

But if on the other hand he believes that God is now visiting the Gentiles not to save the world, but "to take out of them a people for His name" (Acts xv. 14) and that this is the work of the Church in co-operation with the Holy Spirit, then he can be the most optimistic of men, for full well he knows that this work is being accomplished. His goal is the calling out of the Church, the Bride, the Body of Christ.

One will go out to christianize China, an utterly hopeless task; for the Church has never yet christianized one single village or community, let alone a nation. The other will go to co-operate with the Spirit in calling "out" from among the Chinese "a people for His name," the Church. And he will be eminently successful.

There are no Christian nations. What government to-day is guided and controlled by the principle of Jesus? Has the Sermon on the Mount been adopted by the so-called Christian nations as their law? Is there any country in which all are followers of Christ? Then why talk of Christian nations?

War is Hell, sin its author, and selfishness its ruling power. And God declares that it will continue and become more awful until the end of the age, in spite of all men may attempt to do to alter His decrees. Their task is hopeless for the greatest war of all is yet to come. The human heart is to grow worse and worse, not better (1 Tim. iv. 1–3; 2 Tim. iii. 1–5, 13). World Salvation in this age is impossible, and the man who makes that his goal, like a fool, attempts the impossible.

Men used to say that the world was growing better, that there never could be a war again among the Christian (?) nations. To-day they must hang their heads in shame. What have they to answer? How will they explain their position? What now of the German theology which they embraced? They know at last that the world has had a setback and a bad one, too.   Their hopes and ideals have been shattered, and their goal placed farther off.

How will the missionary answer the questions of the Indians? What will he say to the perplexed heathen? Can he explain his past teaching? Is he able yet to prove that the world is growing better, and that Christianity is making progress? Will he stand out still for World-Betterment? They will answer him by pointing to the War, and to the thousands who have lost faith. And he will be dumb.

But if he has taught them according to the Word, if he has told them that they were to expect war; if he has differentiated between the World and the Church, and made it plain that the goal of the Gospel is not the Conversion of the World, but the taking OUT of it a people, the calling out of the Church, and that this the Gospel is surely accomplishing in all lands and among all peoples; if he has been true to the Word, he will have no trouble now. They will understand perfectly, and there will be no pessimism, no discouragement.

The aim of the "New Era" or "Forward Movement," "A Christ-controlled Nation and a Christ-controlled World," was doomed to failure from the beginning because it is absolutely contrary to the Word of God. That is not the mission of the Church nor the aim of the Gospel. Only Jesus Christ Himself can accomplish so great a task. He, the Prince of Peace, must usher in the Millennium.

The vital question is, "Which goal are you working for?" "What do you expect to accomplish?" The roads may start at the same point but they are widely divergent. On one your work is vain, impossible; for the goal you seek does not exist. The world

will not be converted in the present dispensation.
Post-millennialism, or the Conversion of the World
before Christ returns, is a hopeless task. Pre-
millennialism, or the calling OUT of the Church,
for which, when completed, Christ will come, is
the "Blessed Hope" and will be accomplished.
Which is your goal?

CHAPTER XIII

THE INVESTMENT OF LIFE

GOD has a plan for every life. He had a plan for Jeremiah's life even before he saw the light of day (Jer. i. 5). He has a plan for your life; He has one for mine. And because of this fact no one can be supremely happy until he has found God's plan for his life. Are you ever discontented, despondent, or miserable? It may be that you have refused to accept His plan and have persisted in following one of your own. But you ask: "How am I to know God's plan?" That I cannot answer. You must decide it for yourself. I may, however, by God's help, be able to make it easier for you to reach a decision.

As a follower of the Lord Jesus Christ you have but one great aim, i.e., the advancement of God's kingdom. As a Christian, I say, the interests of the kingdom of God become your main object in life. God's work is of paramount importance. Everything else must take a secondary place. Jesus Christ never entrusted this work to the ministers alone; He has laid it upon every Christian man, upon every Christian woman. Each individual believer has his own particular part. God is depending upon you; He is depending upon me. He trusts us. If, then, our aim is to serve the kingdom of God it necessarily follows that

SERVICE IS THE HIGHEST MOTIVE

Not dollars and cents, but service. The man who measures success in life by the standpoint of money has not caught the true meaning of success. There is another standard, vastly higher. Oh, that we might catch the vision of that standard! Let us listen to the warning voice of the Master Himself as He exclaims, "Take heed, and beware of covetousness, for a man's life consisteth not in the abundance of the things which he possesses" (Luke xii. 15).

The majority of you who read this message are intending to spend your lives in the business world. You believe that in this way you can best serve the interests of the kingdom. Probably you are right. It is not for me to act as judge. All that I ask is that you invest your life in terms of service. In other words, if you can best serve God's kingdom as a merchant, then be a merchant; as a lawyer, be a lawyer; as a stenographer, be a stenographer; as a doctor, then by all means be a doctor. God has so ordained it that money is necessary to carry on His work. It may be that He would have you assist in this capacity. But woe unto the man, and woe unto the woman who makes money the aim rather than the means, and piles it up for selfish purposes rather than using it for the glory of God! Beware lest you offer Him money when He is asking for life!

But possibly you are still young. Then to you I would speak especially, for there lies before you a great field of opportunity and responsibility, and you are just on the eve of choosing your life's work. Oh, that I might guide you in your choice! So much depends upon your view of a successful career. You

D

have a life to invest. You desire to invest it as God
has planned you should. But the way seems dark.
There are so many things that you might do that it
seems extremely difficult to decide. Is there no help
in such a crisis, no guiding star? I think there is.
It seems to me that in the investment of life

THE PLACE OF GREATEST NEED HAS FIRST CLAIM

Do we need more business men to-day, or do
we need more ministers, more lawyers or more
foreign missionaries; more doctors in this country
or more in China and India? Do we need more
lady stenographers here, or more workers in the
Far East? We are surely all agreed that the
business world is not suffering as these other places
are. I would turn your eyes to the fields that
are pleading for workers because the need is
greater there than anywhere else.

THE MINISTRY

Take, for instance, the Ministry. How great is
the need here! Oh, young men, do you want a
field of real service, a service that will yield a rich
reward? Then turn to the Ministry. It needs
you, and it may be that you need it. I know of
no calling that gives quite as much joy. Nor have
I ever been sorry that I chose the Ministry as my
life's work.

Why do you not become a minister of the Gospel?
Perhaps that is God's plan for your life. Is it
because it has never occurred to you that you

might? Do you look upon the Ministry as too
high and sacred for you? Then remember that
it is made up of common ordinary men just like
yourself, who have responded to the Call of God.
Or is it because you have been in the habit of
measuring success by the standard of dollars and
cents? I grant you that a minister can never
become rich as a minister. But do you mean
to tell me that D. L. Moody was not a success
simply because he never became wealthy; that
Charles H. Spurgeon's life was a failure because
he died a poor man? God help us to get rid of
such a standard! Success can never be measured
in dollars and cents; it can only be judged in terms
of service. Or is the fault with your parents?
Have they talked before you of making money
until you have come to consider that as the chief
aim of life? God help the parents who place
stumbling-blocks between their sons and the call
of the Ministry!

I would that some of our city men might give
themselves to this glorious work. Why is it that
nearly all our ministers come from the country?
We build large city churches and then go to the
country to get men to fill the pulpits. And yet
the country boy hasn't one-half the advantages
that the city boy enjoys. Most of our men in the
city have known the church from their child-
hood. I seldom had an opportunity, living in
the country, of even attending a church until I
was sixteen; and yet God called me in my boy-
hood days to this, the greatest of all things. Does
it not seem strange? Young men, I ask you to
consider the Ministry before going into business.

THE MISSION FIELD

And now what of the foreign field? I almost hesitate to speak of it; but I must say a few words. And may God help me to say something that will reach every heart!

I take up a book descriptive of the conditions existing in the non-Christian world, and my heart burns within me as I read of the terrible darkness. Two-thirds of the world still without Christ! Thousands dying every day who have never heard the name of Jesus. Africa, "the open sore of the world," with her hundred and fifty millions calling for labourers! India, O poor India! the land of little widows and child-wives, with her three hundred million stretching out weary hands for the Light until she has grown so tired that she doesn't care! And China, the fourth part of the world, absolutely helpless without Christ! O God, how long?

And yet the Saviour's last command was, "Go ye into all the world and preach the Gospel to every creature." Nineteen hundred years have rolled away, and we have not obeyed it yet. O young men, yes, and young women, too, for I speak to you as well, do you want a life of service and sacrifice, but also of untold joy, then I call upon you to respond to the cry that comes from over the seas. You haven't a single talent that God cannot use out there.

If there is one excuse that is given more than another on the part of young women, it is this: "I am needed at home." Or very frequently the mother will say: "Oh, we couldn't possibly

get along without her; we need her at home."
Listen! There comes a time when her hand is
sought in marriage. You give her up. Somehow
she is not needed at home any more; at least
she can be spared and she goes away. What have
you done? You have given her to an earthly
bridegroom, and refused the Heavenly Bridegroom. Jesus, your Saviour—her Saviour—wooed
and won her first. Then He tenderly asked her
to follow Him. You answered: "No, Lord, I
cannot spare her." Later came the earthly
bridegroom, and—well, you know the rest. I
wonder what you will say when you meet Him!
Do you remember that He said: "He that
loveth father or mother more than Me is not
worthy of Me, and he that loveth son or
daughter more than Me is not worthy of Me"?
(Matt. x. 37).

Young men and women, I call you this day to
Christian service. I have only pointed out two
great and needy fields; there are scores of others.
The question resolves itself into this: Are you
willing to accept God's plan for your life? If
so, you will invest your life in terms of service,
and you will endeavour to find the place of greatest
need. Jesus gave up all for us. Is there nothing
we can give to Him? God had only one Son, and
He made Him a missionary. Is there nothing
we can do in return? He Himself has taught us
what it means to be a true disciple when He
says: "If any man will come after Me, let him
deny himself, and take up his cross and follow
Me. For whosoever will save his life shall lose
it; and whosoever will lose his life for My sake
shall find it. For what is a man profited if he

shall gain the whole world, and lose his own
soul?" (Matt. xvi. 24–26).

> Have you heard the Master's Call?
> Will you go, forsaking all?
> Millions still in sin and shame
> Ne'er have heard the Saviour's Name.
>
> Some may give and some may pray,
> But for you He calls to-day;
> Will you answer: "Here am I,"
> Or must Jesus pass you by?
>
> Have you heard their bitter cry?
> Can you bear to see them die,
> Thousands who in darkest night
> Never yet have seen the light?
>
> Soon 'twill be too late to go
> And your love for Jesus show,
> Oh, then, quickly speed away,
> Tarry not another day.
>
> What if you refuse to go?
> Someone then will never know
> Of the Saviour kind and true
> And the blame will rest on you.
>
> Will you, then, forsaking all,
> Gladly heed the Master's Call,
> Answer quickly, "Lord, send me!
> To the lands beyond the sea?"

CHAPTER XIV

OUR MOST IMPORTANT WORK

THE more I study God's Word the more I am convinced that the most important work of the church is the winning of lost men and women to Jesus Christ.

Among many others there are four outstanding passages that clearly set forth this great fact beyond dispute.

First, looking at it from God's side, we find that "Christ Jesus came into the world to save sinners" (1 Tim. i. 15), that "the Son of Man is come to seek and to save that which is lost" (Luke xix. 10). Hence the supreme purpose of Christ's coming to this world was to seek and to save the lost. Not a mission of Social Service and Reformation, but of Salvation and Regeneration.

Then from man's side it is, "to open their eyes, and to turn them from darkness to light, and from the power of Satan unto God" (Acts xxvi. 18). Men are in darkness; they must have their eyes opened and be led into the light. They are under the power of Satan; and hence, they must be delivered and brought to God. Such was Paul's mission.

Then the whole purpose is summed up plainly and unmistakably in Acts xv. 14, where it is stated that God visited the Gentiles "to take out of them a people for His name." That is what God has been doing for the past 1900 years. This is the work of the Holy Spirit to-day. He is gathering out the Body of Christ, His church. From every race and tongue the world over He is calling out this great company.

Now, if such is God's purpose in visiting the Gentiles, and He declares that it is: and if this is the mission of the Holy Spirit in the world, then it is God's will that we should co-operate with Him—for He works through human instruments—and seek to do our part in gathering out His church.

There are some people who shift the responsibility of soul-winning by saying that "one sows and another reaps." Well, suppose you sow a beautiful garden and in the fall of the year some one comes around and sees it. "Now, my friend," he says, "you have done your part, you faithfully did the sowing; and now the time has come for the reaping. I will begin to reap, to gather all these vegetables and this fruit that you have sowed. One sows, you know, and another reaps."

"Oh, no," you exclaim, "I should say not! I sowed this garden for myself. Do you mean to say that I am going to let you have all the fruit of my labour? I will reap it myself." And so you do; for the explanation that "one sows and another reaps," holds good—according to this argument—in the spiritual realm only. What an absurdity!

But God clearly and emphatically states that

it is His will that every servant of His should bear fruit. "I have chosen you and ordained you," He affirms, "that ye should go and bring forth fruit" (John xv. 16). Sometimes I am the one who sows, but at other times I am the one who reaps as well.

If soul-winning is the most important work of the church, it naturally follows that Satan will do all he can to get us side-tracked or satisfied with something else. And such is the case.

Thousands are giving themselves to Social Service, including education, philanthropy and reform work, etc. But Social Service is not Salvation; and Reformation is not Regeneration. One has to do with this life, the other with Eternity. Let us begin at the right end. Get a man saved, and he will soon clean up and reform. It is not our business to improve the world. That is the work of the State. We are to gather out the Church. It is not the outside of the cup and platter alone, but the inside that the Master insists must be clean. Social Service may do for some, but woe to the servant of God who has been called to higher things who is satisfied with it! And the Gospel has not lost its power. Then why waste time?

Multitudes are giving themselves to what is commonly known as church-work. They labour for concerts and bazaars; they are on numerous committees; they are connected with all kinds of organizations, and thus they wear themselves out and think that they are really doing God's service; but they will not spend five minutes in an After-Meeting trying to point souls to Christ. To convince them that they would accomplish a far greater work for God by spending an hour going from door to door distributing Gospel tracts and talking of Jesus than by a week of ticket selling for a concert, would be utterly impossible. So active are they in their "church-work" that they haven't even time to seek and win the lost. May God deliver us from these false ideas regarding His work, and get us concerned with the great realities that confront us as His representatives! For why should we waste our time on non-essentials?

Then when we think of the petty doctrinal controversies that we hear on every side, and see the divisions, the criticisms and jealousies that result therefrom, our hearts grow sick within us; and we would that such trifles might be forgotten in the love and passion for souls, the one power that unites us all. Differences of opinion on unimportant doctrines, questions of church government, and methods of work, etc.—these are the things that divide Christians, rob them of their power, freeze the love of Christ out of their hearts, and kill all passion for souls.

Are we to be united in Heaven and not here? Is it true that we are brothers in Christ? Why then are we so anxious to force our views and interpretations of God's Word upon others? The responsibility rests with each individual to follow the Lord according to the light imparted by the Holy Spirit through the reading of the Word and prayer. Let us remember that there are precious souls to be saved, and that Satan will hinder us if he can; therefore let us be united for their salvation.

Then when we turn to those who are absorbed in the study of prophecy, who preach and teach almost nothing but so-called prophetic truth, forgetful of the fact that prophecy in itself is not the Gospel of Jesus Christ, what a disappointing work we find! How much there is of mere idle speculation! How many different theories of men. Listen! Some of our greatest soul-winners and most successful missionaries have held widely divergent views on the subject of prophetic truth, in spite of which they have maintained the most intimate fellowship with each other because the love of God burned in their hearts and caused them to put first things first.

If we would gauge the spiritual life of a church we must do it by ascertaining its attitude toward the perishing. The Annual Report may tell of a great work done and a large amount of money raised for benevolent purposes, but if it has no record to give of souls won, its spiritual life is low indeed. Bible Conferences may be held and scriptural knowledge imparted, but if the work ends there, it has not been a success from God's standpoint. Men are lost and must be saved and the church that ignores this great fundamental fact is far, far astray. Real spirituality always results in soul winning.

This, then, is our most important work. And what a glorious occupation! How wonderful to be linked up with God in the greatest of all undertakings! Oh, my brethren, let us get back, back to our old-time love for the lost! Where, oh where, is the burden of bygone years! How earnestly we once prayed for perishing souls! How eagerly we watched for results! Have we lost all feeling? Does the awful doom of the unconverted no longer move us! Has Satan so far side-tracked us that we have forgotten our most important work? Oh, then if that be so may God in His great mercy open our eyes, and get us off the side-tracks so cunningly laid by Satan, back to the most important work of the church, the winning of souls to Jesus Christ.

> Lord, send me out with heart aflame
>   To win them to Thy fold;
> Of Jesus and His wondrous love
>   The story must be told.
>
> Lord, send me out, I care not where,
>   With power to win the lost;
> To tell them of redemption free
>   Procured at awful cost.
>
> Lord, send me out, it matters not
>   How hard the task may be;
> The Gospel of Thy Grace, I know,
>   Can set poor sinners free.
>
> Lord, send me out, oh, let me go.
>   I dare not still delay;
> The day of grace will soon be o'er,
>   Then let me speed away.

CHAPTER XV

GO AND TELL OTHERS

IT is eventide. The last lingering ray of the setting sun has sunk below the horizon. The suffocating heat of the day has been replaced by the cooler air of the approaching night. The long, dark shadows cast by the city walls have disappeared. Twilight covers all.

Ever and anon from somewhere within the walls comes a faint plaintive cry. It is probably the cry of a child, caused by the pangs of hunger, for Samaria is undergoing a siege. The Syrians have laid waste the country, and surrounded the city. Days have passed, food has grown scarce, and relief seems farther off than at the beginning.

Upon this particular evening four lepers might have been seen seated on the ground just outside the wall. So weak are they that they can scarcely move. The last scrap of food has been eaten. They have reached their extremity, for when the morrow dawns, it will mean certain death. What are they to do? If they enter the city it will avail them nothing, for food can no longer be had. To remain where they are will mean starvation. Death if they go! Death if they stay! What is to be done? Is there no alternative? Ah, yes! they can give themselves up to the Syrians. True, they may be killed. But then again they may not. It is only a chance in a hundred, but life is dear even to lepers, and they decide to take the chance.

Dragging themselves wearily across the open space as the twilight deepens, they finally reach the outskirts of the camp. All is still and quiet. Not a footstep is heard. What can it mean? Cautiously they make their way from tent to tent. Not a human soul. The Syrians have fled. Yes, fled, and left everything behind them. Food is found in abundance and they are saved.

Like hungry wolves they fall upon the stores, and fairly gorge themselves ere they give any thought to other things. Finally, when they have feasted as only the hungry can, they are suddenly conscience-stricken by the thought of the thousands within the city walls who are dying of starvation while food is within their grasp.

"Then they said one to another, we do not well; this day is a day of good tidings, and we hold our peace; if we tarry till the morning light, punishment will overtake us; now, therefore, come, let us go and tell the King's household" (2 Kings vii. 9). And with hearts grateful for the good things that had come to them, they decided to let the others know. This they did and the city was saved. Hence, our theme, "Go and tell others."

Go and tell others! It is the message that Christ Himself gave to His Church when He said, "Go into all the world and preach the Gospel." It is His will for every Christian. And I believe were He here to-day, in the face of the millions who have never heard His name, His most urgent plea to you and to me would be this: "Go and tell others."

I would urge that we go and tell others first,

BECAUSE OF WHAT WE HAVE

These four lepers had about all they wanted for the present. They had been starving and had been given food. They had been hopeless and had been filled with new aspirations. They had been sad and discouraged; they were now glad and happy. Was it any wonder that they exclaimed, "We do not well; this day is a day of good tidings, and we hold our peace."

But brethren, what had they in comparison to what you and I have in Jesus Christ? Their salvation was physical and temporal. Ours is spiritual and eternal. They had been freed from the pangs of hunger. We have been freed from the power of sin. Think of it!—forgiven, our hearts cleansed by the blood of Jesus Christ, the presence of God ever with us, joy, peace, comfort, the hope of life beyond the grave, re-union with those we loved and lost awhile, heaven with all its glories, and best of all Jesus Christ Himself, our Comforter in sorrow, our Guide in the darkness, and our Strength and Hope in death. Surely, surely we have something worth giving to others! Are we going to be selfish? Would we keep it all for ourselves? Or will we do as these poor lepers did for a starving city? Will we go and tell others?

But if we should tell others because of what we have, then surely it is our duty to go and tell others.

BECAUSE OF WHAT THEY NEED

Within the walls of Samaria were literally thousands of men and women dying of hunger. So dire was the situation, so pressing the need, that mothers were cooking their own sons that they might live a little longer. Could we imagine a greater need? Food was worth its weight in gold, and it was food they needed. And the lepers, knowing it, decided to go and tell them of their deliverance.

My friends, there are men and women on every side who are perishing for the Bread of Life, and we are able to supply their need. It may be that the man who works by our side day after day does not know Jesus Christ, and we have never told him. Take, for instance, the friends with whom we associate. We, ourselves, have heard the "Glad Tidings" and Jesus has become our Saviour. But what of them? Have we ever told them what Jesus means to us? Have we ever tried to supply their need?

Far away in Africa, India, China, and Japan, there are millions of precious souls for whom He died. And yet they have never heard His name. They are starving for the Good News. Their homes are often wretched hovels. They get but three or four meals a week in many cases. Famine has stalked across their lands leaving disease and death in its wake. Immorality is sanctioned by their religion, and idols are their gods. They live in constant dread of evil spirits and demons of every description. Their religions give them no hope. Life itself is a burden. Would that I could paint the need! Oh, for the brush of a Raphael or the skill of a Michel Angelo that I might picture the degradation, that I might reveal their distress! And yet we have it. Think of it, men and women, we have what they lack! Shall we go and tell them? Surely they need us! The last great command of the One whom we love and serve was "Go." And yet nineteen centuries have rolled away, and still the world is unevangelized. They perish, perish for want of light. Shall we go and tell others?

And last of all we must go and tell others.

BECAUSE THERE IS DANGER IF WE FAIL

I mean danger to ourselves. Hear the warning as we turn to our text: "If we tarry till the morning light punishment will overtake us." Ah, yes! They dare not tarry. They dare not withhold the "Glad Tidings." Some kind of punishment would surely overtake them if they did. And so without any more hesitation they went at once to tell others.

The Gospel has come to us, and through the atoning blood of Jesus Christ we are saved. But listen, we keep it at our peril. We must either go backward or forward. We cannot stand still. The secret of growth in the Christian life is activity. If we lie down and do nothing for Christ we will grow weaker and weaker, colder and colder, until at last our interest will be all gone, and we our-

selves will drift from the Church back into the
world where our last state will be worse than our
first. One of the greatest prerequisites of the
Christian life is service. We must go to work for
Christ. We were not saved for what we could get
out of it; we were not saved merely that we might
escape hell and get to heaven. That is pure selfishness. No! No! We were saved to serve, and
unless we find something to do we will die of
inaction. If I do not use my muscles I will
soon find that I cannot. The Hindoo ascetic
who holds his arm in the air for a number of
weeks finds that he can never bring it down
again.

There are thousands of Christians, I am sorry
to say, who never speak a word for their Master.
In the testimony meeting they are silent, though
their tongues fly fast enough at home. They can
talk to their fellow men, but somehow when it
comes to speaking for God they are utterly and
hopelessly dumb. They have loved ones in their
own homes who do not know Christ, and yet they
are afraid to say a word to them. Loud enough
in most things, but silent when it comes to Christianity. God pity them! Ashamed of Christ! And
some day they will find Christ ashamed of them.
The fact is they do not really believe that their
friends and loved ones are lost. If they did they
would never rest day or night until they were
saved. How could they? Oh, why is it so? Why
this selfishness?

If we have found joy in Christ, why shouldn't
we tell others? If we know in our hearts that our
loved ones are lost and that they will be shut out
of heaven and separated from us through all eter-

nity, tell me, why do we not ask them to accept Jesus Christ?

Unless we go and tell others we ourselves will grow cold and indifferent. Our reward will go to another, and we will suffer unutterable loss. "When I say unto the wicked, thou shalt surely die; and thou givest him not warning, nor speakest to warn the wicked from his wicked way, to save his life; the same wicked man shall die in his iniquity; but his blood will I require at thine hand" (Ezek. iii. 18). Oh, how solemn the warning, "his blood will I require at thine hand!"

"We do not well," exclaimed the lepers, "this day is a day of good tidings, and we hold our peace: if we tarry till the morning light, punishment will overtake us; now, therefore come, let us go and tell the king's household." Oh, my brethren, let us also go and tell others, even as the four lepers went. The world is dying for our message. Souls are perishing without Christ. It is for each one of us to go and tell others.

> Go and tell the joy of Jesus!
>   Tell it out where e'er you go;
> Sing, oh, sing of His redemption,
>   Banish sorrow, pain and woe!
>
> Go and tell the joy of Jesus!
>   Tell of how He bled and died;
> Souls are waiting to receive Him,
>   Jesus Christ the Crucified.
>
> Go and tell the joy of Jesus!
>   It will thrill another heart;
> He is waiting now to enter,
>   And the light of Life impart.

Go and tell the joy of Jesus!
  Let the whole, wide world behold
In your life the wondrous vision
  Of a joy and peace untold.

Go and tell the joy of Jesus!
  Let it echo far and wide;
All around you hearts are aching,
  Hearts for whom He bled and died.

CHAPTER XVI

CHRIST'S THREEFOLD COMMISSION

IN Christ's threefold Commission we have the complete programme of missionary enterprise for this dispensation. This threefold Commission is expressed in three simple words.

LOOK

"Say ye not, There are yet four months and then cometh harvest? behold, I say unto you, Lift up your eyes, and look on the fields; for they are white already to harvest" (John iv. 35).

Thousands have no vision or knowledge of the need; hence great sums are wasted on expensive church buildings and equipment, while millions perish without even a mud hut in which to hear the Good News. One real look through the eyes of Jesus Christ and we will sink our funds not in bricks and mortar, luxurious Bible Training Schools and expensive institutions, but in the souls of men. Tabernacles and halls will suffice for our places of worship that the "other sheep" may also have a part. Non-necessities will give place to needs, luxuries dispensed with, personal and selfish gratification most carefully guarded, and life henceforth lived for those who have never heard. That is, if our hearts are moved with the compassion of Jesus and our eyes anointed to see as He saw.

Oh, then, let us look; look as we have never looked before. And as we see in vision the teeming millions of China and India with the benighted multitudes of Africa and South America, let us listen again to the Master's words and catch a glimpse of the urgency of the need. "Behold, I say unto you, Lift up your eyes, and look on the fields; for they are white already to harvest."

Have you ever seen a harvest in our great Canadian Northwest? Then you know what it means. How urgent! How important that labourers be rushed off in train-loads. And why? Simply because the harvest must be gathered at once or it will be lost, and lost forever.

So it is with the whitened fields of souls. This generation can only evangelize this generation. Therefore, "What thou doest do quickly." If labourers do not hurry off at once, if we fail to do our utmost, this harvest, this generation will be lost forever.

Yes, and this may be our last opportunity to show Him how much we love Him. Some of us may soon be gone, for "the night cometh when no man can work." For many "the day is far spent." There are those who up to the present have lived for self and self alone. And now their years are numbered. Never yet have they manifested their love to Jesus Christ in any worth while way. Oh, then, let us be up and doing. Our last opportunity will soon be gone. In God's name, let us lift up our eyes and look, look on the fields white already to harvest!

PRAY

Humanly speaking the task is absolutely impossible. There are more heathen to-day than there were a century ago in spite of what we have done. What is the solution? "Money," replies one. "Let us gather together millions of dollars and we can evangelize the world." "Men," answers another. "Give us sufficient men to go and we will accomplish the task in this generation." No, friend, that is not God's method. Neither money nor men will do it.

Listen: "The harvest truly is plenteous, but the labourers are few." There you have the difficulties of the task, a great harvest and an inadequate number of harvesters. But hark! The Master continues to speak. Thank God, He has the solution and the problem is solved. "Pray ye therefore the Lord of the harvest, that He will send forth labourers into His harvest" (Matt. ix. 37–38).

We have by far too many labourers now, labourers, I mean, of the wrong kind. They do not know their business, nor how to garner in the ripened harvest. With their Modern Theology and Social-uplift ideas they have sought to do what can never be done. Would to God they could be sent home! What a blessing it would be to countless thousands! Our business is to "pray the Lord of the harvest, that He will send forth labourers." And when God sends men He always sends the right kind. This then is the secret—PRAY.

GO

1. *To the Nations.*

"Go ye therefore and teach all nations" (Matt. xxviii. 19).

The Bridegroom must have some from every tongue and tribe. "A great multitude, which no man could number, of all nations, and kindreds, and people, and tongues, stood before the throne" (Rev. vii. 9). This is borne out in Acts xv. 14, "God did visit the Gentiles to take out of them a people for His Name." Hence, we have in Mark xiii. 10 these prophetic words: "And the Gospel must first be published among all nations," with the promise in Matthew, "and then shall the end come." Therefore, "Why speak ye not a word of bringing back the king?" This Paul declared to be his aim, namely, "To preach the Gospel in the Regions Beyond" (2 Cor. x. 16). Such, too was the plan of Jesus Himself. "All men seek for Thee," they told Him. "Let us go into the next towns that I may preach there also" (Mark i. 35–39) was His answer. And in Luke iv. 43 He is even more emphatic. "I must preach the Kingdom of God to other cities also: for therefore am I sent," He insisted. Then in Acts i. 8 we are definitely commissioned to a worldwide testimony, even "unto the uttermost part of the earth."

This, then, is to be our vision. Not the duplicating of existing missionary agencies; rather we are to work in places still untouched. "Unoccupied Areas," "where Christ has not been named," "the Regions Beyond," "farther, still farther into the night," "the Neglected Fields." These are our watchwords, this our glorious mission.

2. *To the Individual.*

"Go ye into all the world, and preach the Gospel to every creature" (Mark xvi. 15).

This is our responsibility and obligation to the individual. "When I say unto the wicked, thou shalt surely die; and thou givest him not warning, nor speakest to warn the wicked from his wicked way, to save his life; the same wicked man shall die in his iniquity; but his blood will I require at thine hand" (Ezek. iii. 18). What about the guilt of the man who finds a broken rail, but neglects to flag the train; or the one who watches a blind man about to fall over a precipice and neglects to call; or the one who sees another drowning and neglects to reach out a hand; or the one who notices a house on fire and neglects to give the alarm?

We have now been brought face to face with an individual responsibility. And again the awful question, "Am I my brother's keeper?" demands an answer. "Every creature." These are the Master's words. We will have to get back to the anointed vision of Dr. A. B. Simpson, when he wrote:

> " A hundred thousand souls a day,
>   Are passing one by one away,
>   In Christless guilt and gloom;
> Without one ray of hope or light,
> With future dark as endless night,
>   They're passing to their doom."

Oh, child of God, what are you doing? What have you done? How will you face them? What will you say when they meet you up Yonder? Can you bear the thought? Your Master's Commission, clear, plain and emphatic, the appalling need brought before you again and again, and yet you never raised a hand. The plate was passed and almost indifferently you tossed on a ten dollar bill, and that was the measure of your interest for a whole year. With that your duty to missions ended. And you spend more in one week on yourself. God have mercy on you!

> " O Church of Christ, what wilt thou say
> When in the awful judgment day,
> They charge thee with their doom?"

How much treasure have you laid up in heaven? Where are your riches? In some earthly bank, where you must part with them sooner or later? Or have you consumed all on yourself? If such is the case you will enter heaven a poor man. Think of it! A pauper in heaven. No one to meet you because no investment in souls. God help us to store up treasure in heaven by investing in precious souls here. "Lay not up for yourselves treasures upon earth, but lay up for yourselves treasures in heaven" (Matt. vi. 19). This is the command of Jesus Christ. Are we prepared to obey?

Do you know that one hundred dollars a year for missions is less than two dollars per week? Think of it! What is your salary? Fifteen, twenty-five, forty dollars a week? Then that means thirteen, twenty-three or thirty-eight dollars each week on yourself, and only the paltry sum of two dollars for the evangelization of the world. What a crime! What an unequal division!

I will never forget a young woman who is now in Glory, Grace, by name. She was converted in my meetings and her heart was soon after set on fire for the "other sheep." Her mother had promised her a new overcoat. The one she had failed many a time to keep out the piercing cold. It had been worn six years. Yet Grace, whose heart was in the foreign field, finally persuaded her mother to let her wear the old coat one more winter, and to give her the money for missions. Talk about sacrifice! How little we know! But that was not all, for when Grace lay on her deathbed she made her mother promise to sell her clothes and send the money to the Regions Beyond. I would like to be somewhere near when Grace receives her reward. What a sight it will be! Oh, how rich she was toward God!

Beloved, I am done! My message has been given. The responsibility now rests upon you. What are you going to do about it? What is your part? Christ's Threefold Commission has now been set before you. Look! Pray. Go! You can look and you can pray. And if you cannot go, you can make it possible for those to go whom God in answer to prayer would thrust forth into the whitened harvest fields.

Hark! the Master calleth: "Who for Me will go?"
Some from every nation must the Saviour know;
"Other sheep" are waiting for the Gospel Call,
Every tongue must praise Him—Jesus died for all.

Harvest fields are bending, soon 'twill be too late,
Reapers now are needed, lo! 'tis death to wait;
Who will take the Gospel over land and sea?
Who will answer gladly: "Here am I, send me"?

All may share the glory, some can give and pray,
Others at His bidding quickly speed away;
Life must be invested, none for self may live,
Who will heed the challenge, all for Jesus give?

Hasten, then, oh hasten, to the lands of night,
Farther and still farther with the gospel Light;
Every tribe and nation has a right to hear,
This the great Commission—Jesus made it clear.

CHAPTER XVII

OUR TWOFOLD TASK

IT is necessary that we have very clear and definite views regarding our responsibility. Not only must we do God's work; it must be done in His way. Our greatest danger perhaps is that of multiplying organizations and broadening our mission until the important and essential task for which we exist has been either lost sight of or is entirely crowded out.

So far as the work is concerned we have no difficulty. Our instructions are clear. In Acts vi. 4, we have these words: "We will give ourselves continually to prayer and to the ministry of the Word." Our first task, therefore, is "prayer" without which all our work will be ineffective. And the second to which we are called is "the ministry of the Word."

In Acts i. 8 we are designated as the Lord's "witnesses" and in Mark xvi. 15 our instructions are unmistakable: "Go ye into all the world and preach the Gospel to every creature." And again, "Preach the Word" (2 Tim. iv. 2).

If we are true to these two tasks, viz., "intercession" and "witness-bearing," we will have our hands more than full.

Our prayer obligation will be discharged both privately and publicly; while the Word can be ministered "to every creature" in several different ways. It can be proclaimed from the pulpit; it can be done through personal work, individual to individual; it can be ministered through the distribution of Gospel tracts, etc.

To be true to our twofold task will mean the elimination of all machinery, organization and activity that does not accomplish God's definitely stated work. While, on the other hand, the introduction of these things is bound to obscure the vision and crowd out this great twofold task which has been committed to the church.

> I have seen the vision,
>   And for self I cannot live;
> Life is less than worthless
>   Till my all I give.